# THE
# VINTNER'S TABLE
## COOKBOOK

# THE
# VINTNER'S
# TABLE
## COOKBOOK

### Recipes from a
### Winery Chef

MARY EVELY

# The Vintner's Table Cookbook

Published by Simi Winery
© Copyright 1998 by Simi Winery

# S I M I

Project Director: Nancy Gilbert
Recipe development and food styling: Mary Evely
Photography: M.J. Wickham

Edited, designed and manufactured in the United States of America by
Favorite Recipes® Press, an imprint of

FRP

2451 Atrium Way
Nashville, Tennessee 37214

Book Design: Steve Newman
Managing Editor: Mary Cummings
Project Editor: Jane Hinshaw
Production Manager: Mark Sloan
Project Production: Sara Anglin

Library of Congress Number: 97-061141
ISBN: 0-9658718-0-0
First printing: 1998  15,000 copies

Any inquiries or orders for additional copies of this book
should be directed to:

Simi Winery
P O Box 698
Healdsburg, CA 95448
Telephone: 707/433-6981
FAX: 707/433-6253

# FOREWORD

There is no doubt that the meals we recall most fondly were made memorable both by the company at the table and by the happy combination of foods and wines. Good food and good wine are natural companions, but creating those memorable meals yourself is difficult unless you know what makes food and wine taste good together.

The serious study of how wines pair best with different foods has, for the most part, been undertaken either haphazardly or intuitively, with no available explanation of the pairing principles that can be easily grasped and used by the average person.

Simi Chef Mary Evely, in a thirteen-year-long series of food and wine pairing meals sponsored by Simi Winery, has studied, questioned, and explored why certain flavors and textures of food pair beautifully with some wines and are lost with others. Using her artist's eye, palate, and sensibility, she has developed simple principles for the successful pairing of good wine and good food.

The Vintner's Table Cookbook is the happy result of Mary's work at Simi's Vintner's Table. It will allow anyone to pair good food and wine with a minimum of effort, and yet offer a depth of information to those with further interest in the subject. Mary shares with you her best recipes—recipes based on simple, fresh ingredients, most of which you can easily find in season at your local supermarket.

Each recipe is matched to the wine varietal that suits it best and is arranged in chapters organized by wine varietal: Chardonnay, Sauvignon Blanc, blush wines, Pinot Noir, Zinfandel, and Cabernet Sauvignon. And, of course, the dessert hounds at Simi made sure that she added a dessert chapter featuring sparkling and sweet wines! So if you know that you are serving a bottle of Pinot Noir with dinner this evening, you can simply turn to the chapter on Pinot Noir and find recipes that all work beautifully with that varietal.

As both Winemaker and then President at Simi, I have been fortunate to observe, learn from, and enjoy Mary's work, and to savor her delicious, beautiful dishes, impeccably harmonized with our wines. Now you can enjoy them, too. Bon appetit!

*Zelma Long*

C O N T

E    N    T    S

# PREFACE

Like most Americans, I did not grow up with wine. When I was first living and cooking on my own, I had the good fortune to discover James Beard and Julia Child. Their books inspired in me a love and respect for good food that has continued to grow over the years. Once immersed in the wonderful world of taste, it wasn't long before I became curious about wine. At that time, I think Julia's books were the only ones that gave wine recommendations for recipes, but, since the books were on the subject of French cooking, all the recommended wines were, naturally, French. But American winemakers were beginning to make their mark, and it was tasting a California Chardonnay that gave me my first experience of a really good wine.

Within two years, I was living in California, where I continued my self-education in the world of food and wine. Eventually, my passion for the subject led me to change my avocation into a vocation, and I began working for Simi Winery in Sonoma County. I created a food and wine program for Simi called The Vintner's Table, a place where everyone could learn about the pleasures of the table.

I have spent over ten years researching and learning about how food and wine interact. This book is the result. It is organized around the most popular American wine varieties, the wines we drink most often. If the concepts in the recipes interest you, there is additional information in the "Principles of Food and Wine Pairing" in the front of the book. In addition, each chapter has a "Profile" page for that variety, with a description of the wine and how it works with food. Look also for the recipes marked with a ✿. These are what I call Chameleon Recipes because, with minor changes, they can work with more than one wine.

From my years of working with food and wine, I have realized a great pleasure beyond that of the palate. Sharing the pleasures of the table instills admiration for the work of the people and the land that provides good honest food, brings good cheer, and makes friends around the world. I have been so rewarded. I wish the same for you.

*Mary Evely*

8

This book is dedicated,
with thanks,
to all the people who tasted
and learned along with me at
The Vintner's Table;
and to all the chefs who have
worked in my kitchen,
helping me develop
a wine-friendly cuisine.

# INFLUENCES ON THE PALATE

Food is food and wine is wine, but magic can happen when you combine the two. Each is changed by the other. Three main things affect our perception of foods and wines—flavor, texture, and external influences, or influences outside the interaction of textures and flavors on the palate.

## FLAVOR

When winemakers sat down to analyze their wines, they discovered how difficult it is to describe a flavor. Anne Noble, a professor in the Department of Viticulture and Enology at the University of California at Davis addressed this problem by creating the Wine Aroma Wheel. Since 90 percent of flavor perception comes from aroma, it is extremely helpful in zeroing in on that familiar flavor that you can't quite identify. Pinpointing flavors in wines in this manner can guide you to some good food choices.

### Matching Flavors

Similarity of flavors between wine and food makes for pleasant combinations. Echo a flavor component of a wine by using it in the food: the black currant flavors in Cabernet, for instance, can be matched by using black currant liqueur in a sauce.

### Matching Flavor Intensity

Flavors in foods and wines can range from subtle and delicate to very big and powerful. To fully appreciate the combination of food and wine flavors, it is important to match the intensity of the two. Delicate wines are best enjoyed with delicately flavored dishes; rich and powerful wines go best with big flavors in the food. For instance, a full-flavored reserve-style Chardonnay would overwhelm the delicate flavors of fillet of sole, but this wine is wonderful with roast veal or pork.

# FOOD AND

# WINE AROMA WHEEL

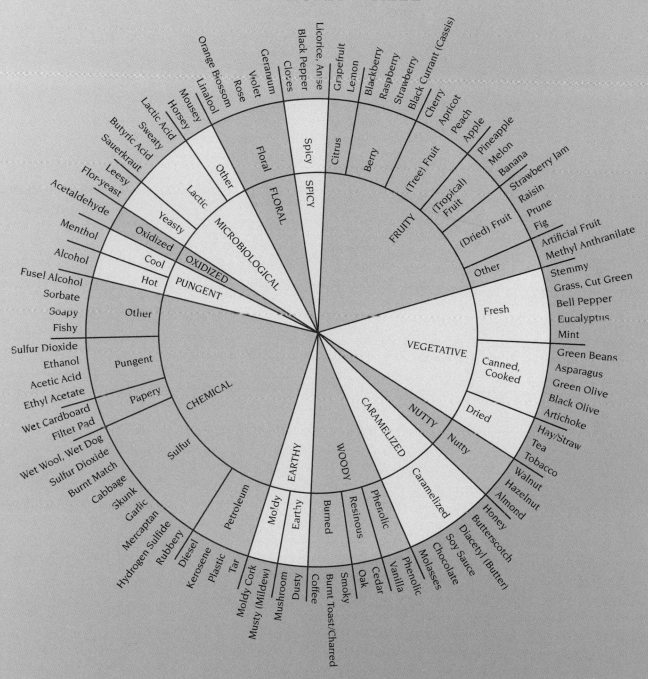

# WINE PAIRING

# Texture

Texture is the tactile experience your tongue has when it encounters the sensations of sweet, sour, salty, bitter, and fat. It accounts for the other 10 percent of flavor perception. Sweet, sour, salty, and bitter all have specific sites of recognition on the tongue and palate. Sweet is recognized at the tip of the tongue, sour at the sides, salty in the center, and bitter at the base. Fat coats the palate, reducing its ability to perceive the other four textures. Because textures are recognized on a very basic level of the senses, their influence will often be stronger than that of specifically defined flavors.

## Balancing Textures

An imbalance of wine and food textures can make an excellent wine taste terrible. Consider the textures of a wine and the elements in the dish that you propose to serve with it. The following guidelines will help ensure success:

> *Sweet (Fruit and/or Sugar)* - The sweetness of a dish should always be lesser, or more subtle, than the sweetness of the wine that accompanies it. Otherwise, the palate cannot perceive the fruit in the wine and it appears thin, tart, and/or bitter.

> *Sour (Acid)* - Always make sure that the acid levels in a dish, such as a salad with a vinaigrette, are lesser than that of the wine. If you lose the perception of the acid in wine, it will seem flat or dull.

> *Salty* - Salt and acid work very well in opposition. As a result, salty foods go very well with high-acid wines; think about smoked salmon with Sauvignon Blanc or Champagne. Salt also opposes bitter, reducing the perception of tannin or bitterness in food or wine.

> *Bitter (Tannin)* - Bitter foods such as oil-cured olives will diminish the perception of bitterness or astringency from the tannins in young red wines, allowing you the full impact of the varietal fruit flavors.

> *Fat* - Cheese is often served at red wine tastings, because the fat in the cheese coats the palate and lessens the perception of tannic or bitter flavors. High-fat foods generally require the intensity of rich, intense, "fat" wines to balance them.

### Hot Spices as a Texture Consideration

Uncooked garlic, horseradish, hot mustard, black pepper, and chili peppers all have the capability of burning, or numbing, the palate, making it less able to perceive the subtle flavors in wine. Some of these, horseradish and mustard in particular, seem to "burn" in the sinuses and disperse fairly rapidly, leaving the palate ready for the next sip of wine. Peppers, however, particularly chili peppers, can numb the palate long enough to make them poor companions of wine.

An interesting test for hot flavors in regard to wine compatibility is to apply the ingredient to the skin. If you can feel the heat, it is definitely too hot for the full enjoyment of wine.

## CONTRASTING FLAVORS AND TEXTURES

Sometimes brilliant combinations can be made by using contrasting, rather than similar, flavors or textures. This is quite tricky, as there are no hard-and-fast guidelines for what might work and what will not, other than the salt-acid contrast discussed previously in the Salty category of textures.

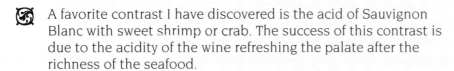 A favorite contrast I have discovered is the acid of Sauvignon Blanc with sweet shrimp or crab. The success of this contrast is due to the acidity of the wine refreshing the palate after the richness of the seafood.

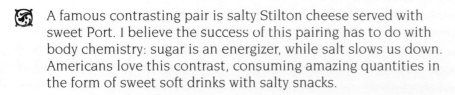 A famous contrasting pair is salty Stilton cheese served with sweet Port. I believe the success of this pairing has to do with body chemistry: sugar is an energizer, while salt slows us down. Americans love this contrast, consuming amazing quantities in the form of sweet soft drinks with salty snacks.

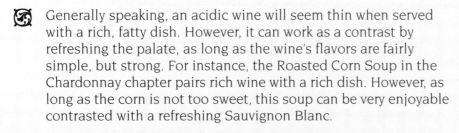 Generally speaking, an acidic wine will seem thin when served with a rich, fatty dish. However, it can work as a contrast by refreshing the palate, as long as the wine's flavors are fairly simple, but strong. For instance, the Roasted Corn Soup in the Chardonnay chapter pairs rich wine with a rich dish. However, as long as the corn is not too sweet, this soup can be very enjoyable contrasted with a refreshing Sauvignon Blanc.

Contrast is a fascinating area for continued testing. All adventurous cooks and diners are encouraged to try some experiments in this field. It's a thrill when you make a successful discovery of your own.

13

# COLOR: FOOD AND WINE PAIRING WITH AN ARTIST'S EYE

One of my jobs as Chef of Simi Winery is to compile lists of food affinities for each variety of wine that Simi produces. In the course of describing such a list for Cabernet Sauvignon, I realized that there was a color harmonic in all the food: black pepper; char from grilling; dark-fleshed meat, poultry and fish; and dark grains such as lentils and wild rice. I began imagining a beautiful still-life of these foods, all in harmonic dark colors. That led me to thinking that every wine variety might have a specific color harmonic with food. This is clearly not scientific, and it doesn't work 100 per cent of the time, but it is a tool that has led me to some exciting food and wine pairings that I might never have thought of otherwise. This is how I discovered the affinities among other things for roses and blush wines, and the golden saffron with Chardonnay. I have found it to be consistent enough that I could determine a particular color for each wine variety that I studied and to suggest them as a color code for the chapters in this book.

*Blush wines* - pink (strawberries, raspberries, roses, ham, smoked meats)

*Sauvignon Blanc* - green (green herbs, lettuces, green vegetables)

*Chardonnay* - golden yellow (butter, corn, mild curry, chanterelles)

*Pinot Noir* - purple-red (beets, pomegranates, red chard, squab)

*Zinfandel* - rust-red (dried tomatoes, barbecue, chili, paprika, sausage)

*Cabernet Sauvignon* - black (black rice, black pepper, morels, black currants)

Following a color trail provides ideas for exciting new food affinities, as well as beautiful garnishes and plate presentations.

# OTHER INFLUENCES

There are many differences of opinion on the subject of food and wine pairing that result from influences besides taste and aroma.

## Temperature

The temperature at which a wine is served greatly affects the experience of it. Cold temperatures decrease perception of flavor on the palate, and dishes which are to be served cold must be more highly seasoned to be enjoyable. A dry white wine served ice cold will seem almost flavorless, but will reveal layers of flavor as it warms. Serving wines at too warm a temperature will make them seem highly alcoholic and rough.

Your perception of the temperature of the weather, the room, and your own body will also influence the varietal that you want to drink and the temperature at which you want to drink it.

### Mood/Occasion

Your sense of occasion will often make one wine seem like the best choice, when, in fact, more than one might actually work well with the food. Celebrations seem to call for Champagne with oysters, even though you usually choose a Sauvignon Blanc to serve with bivalves. Or, if you have been working really hard in the garden and you're tired and grimy, it seems time for a refreshing, uncomplicated bottle of Rosé with a grilled sausage sandwich. Yet that same sandwich, when shared with friends at a social supper, makes you reach for the Cabernet Sauvignon.

### Body Chemistry

There is no doubt that we use chemistry in both wine-making and cooking. There is also a chemical process taking place from the moment we put the food and wine into our mouths. If you have just spent a weekend on a gastronomic tour, wining and dining at every meal, the idea of lobster in butter sauce with a big, rich Chardonnay may not seem very appealing. On the other hand, if you have been watching your fat intake and exercising faithfully, it could taste fabulous as a special splurge. And consider how your taste perceptions and preferences go haywire when you are sick.

### Quality

The better a wine is, the broader the range of foods with which it will be compatible. The flaws in a lesser bottle will be pointed up by any ingredient that is not in perfect harmony with the variety.

### Personal Preference (The first and last principle)

What you like best is always best. No matter how well Gewürztraminer goes with Choucroute Garni or other sauerkraut dishes, if you don't like Gewürztraminer, you're not going to like the combination. This will be an unending battle with your Gewürztraminer-loving friends.

## CHAMELEON FOODS AND RECIPES

Some ingredients are just naturally wine-friendly. They can go with a broad range of wines, depending on the cooking method or other ingredients in the recipe. Garlic and onions both fall into this category, as do parsley and basil. In fact, I can't think of a wine that would clash with onions in some form or another, so I have not listed them specifically in the individual lists of food affinities. Chameleon recipes are those that can, with minor alterations, be made to work with more than one wine. They are marked throughout the book with this grape leaf symbol.

# ANALYZING RECIPES FOR WINE

Once you have used the food affinities lists at the beginning of each chapter for a while, you will begin to have a sense about what works for each wine variety. Scanning the ingredients list for a recipe may be enough to suggest an appropriate wine. Since food and wine pairing is a fairly new subject, however, you may often find recipes which pose problems for the choice of wine. Below is an ingredients list from a recipe selected at random from A *Taste of San Francisco*, a fund-raising cookbook for the San Francisco Symphony:

6 chicken breast halves
2 eggs
all-purpose flour for dredging
1 1/4 cups freshly grated Parmesan cheese
5 to 6 tablespoons chopped fresh tarragon
2 tablespoons chopped chervil
1/2 to 3/4 cup clarified butter
1 1/2 tablespoons chopped shallots
5 to 6 tablespoons chopped fresh parsley
5 to 6 capers, drained
6 to 8 tablespoons butter
1 pound haricots verts or asparagus

I was sure that this recipe was going to be a winner for Chardonnay, with the butter, cheese and sweet herbs of tarragon and chervil. Then I got to the capers. The acids of these pickled buds would wreak havoc on a Chardonnay, overwhelming the refreshing acid balance of the wine and leaving it flat and dull on the palate. Insult is added to injury by adding haricots verts or asparagus, with their green vegetal flavors, which fight with the soft fruity character of Chardonnay. The solution would be to substitute sliced green onions or chives for the capers, which would give a fresh lift to the richness of the dish without competing with the wine. For the vegetable, either spinach or green cabbage would provide the color contrast without the strong vegetal flavors of green beans or asparagus.

The key when reviewing a recipe for wine affinity is that all the ingredients should be on the same harmonic for a particular wine variety. As the above example demonstrates, it is often a simple matter to make adjustments to a recipe to make this alignment. Sometimes it is only a matter of determining which variety would best suit a recipe, using the wine profiles and food and wine-pairing principles as a guide.

For another example, consider the ingredients list for a dish from *Savoring the Wine Country*, compiled and edited by Meesha Halm and Dayna Macy—a very nice book, by the way. A soup recipe, which the chef has paired with a dry, grassy Sauvignon Blanc, calls for the following ingredients:

1 onion
1 leek
2 red beets
1 quart water, chicken stock or vegetable stock
2 tablespoons thyme leaves
6 cloves garlic
2 ears white corn
$1^{1}/_{2}$ quarts half-and-half
salt and freshly ground white pepper
low-fat yogurt for garnishing

Scanning the recipe, all of the ingredients are on a Sauvignon Blanc harmonic, except the beets. They are characterized by sweet, earthy flavors which make them ideal with a fruity Pinot Noir, but a conflict with the grassy acidity of Sauvignon Blanc. In addition, the directions call for roasting the corn directly over a flame until the kernels begin to blacken. The flavors resulting in that charring also take this in a red wine direction. To make this recipe work better with Sauvignon Blanc, I would substitute yellow tomatoes for the beets and cut the corn off the cob to add it uncooked to the soup.

Try this little test. My friend Kathleen Taggart created a wonderful mushroom tart recipe for *Entertaining People*, a cookbook she co-authored with her fellow instructors at a Portland, Oregon, cooking school. Look at the ingredients list and see if you get an idea for a good wine match for this recipe. The filling ingredients, which go into a poppy seed short crust are:

$^{1}/_{2}$ ounce dried porcini mushrooms
$^{1}/_{2}$ pound fresh mushrooms
$^{1}/_{2}$ medium onion
2 tablespoons chopped fresh sage
3 large eggs
$1^{1}/_{2}$ cups heavy cream
$^{1}/_{2}$ teaspoon kosher salt
$^{1}/_{4}$ pound goat cheese

If you are thinking Chardonnay, you have the picture. In this case, with the very richly flavored porcini and the pungent sage, I would look for a big, rich, oak-barrel-aged version to balance the intensity of flavors.

# CREATING WINE MENUS

When tasting several wines, we begin with the simplest, most delicate and refreshing varieties, and end with the most intensely flavored, rich and complex wines. It would be difficult to perceive the flavors in a delicate wine after tasting a rich, heavy one. The same idea applies to planning a menu. Each course will be enjoyed to its fullest if you start with more delicate dishes when your palate and appetite are fresh, and stimulate with the richer, full-flavored dishes as the palate begins to tire.

It is also best to vary the textures and flavors from course to course, avoiding, for instance, placing a cream soup on the same menu as a crème brûlée for dessert. The idea is to keep delighting the palate with the variety and progressive intensity and complexity of flavors.

### A Multi-Course Menu for Winter

Smoked Trout Mousse with Belgian Endive
*Sauvignon Blanc*

Roasted Pumpkin Risotto with Fresh Sage
*Chardonnay*

Rack of Lamb with White Bean Purée
*Cabernet Sauvignon or Merlot*

Apple Galettes
*Late Harvest White Wine*

### A Multi-Course Menu for Summer

Raspberry Rose Salad
*Rosé*

Grilled Scallops with Sweet Pepper Relish
*Sauvignon Blanc*

Beef Brochettes with Black-Eyed Peas
*Pinot Noir*

Our Favorite Cookies

Iced Coffee or Tea

Generally, we serve a progression of courses and wines as just described only for special occasions and grand celebrations. On the other hand, any time you have four to six people, try serving two different wines, rather than two bottles of the same wine. It will add variety and interest to the meal, as well as provide the opportunity to try something new.

### A Two-Wine Menu for Spring

Rock Shrimp Remoulade with Grilled Asparagus
*Sauvignon Blanc*

Spinach Pasta with Chicken and Pancetta
*Chardonnay*

Polenta Fruit Cobbler

Coffee or Tea

### A Two-Wine Menu for Winter

Roasted Onion and Garlic Bisque
*Chardonnay*

Roast Duck Leg with Pomegranate
*Pinot Noir*

Chocolate Napoleons

Coffee or Tea

Sometimes you are just in the mood for one particular wine, or there is just you or the two of you for the meal, and you won't need more than one bottle. In this case, simply choose dishes that are all in harmony with that wine, providing the interest and variety with colors, textures, and a good range of ingredients.

### A One-Wine Menu for Summer

Panzanella - Bread and Tomato Salad

Salmon with Saffron Sauce
*Chardonnay*

Peach and Raspberry Gratin

### A One-Wine Menu for Autumn

Green Salad with Sun-Dried Tomato Vinaigrette

Cioppino - Seafood Stew
*Zinfandel*

Chili-Lime Sorbet

# SERVING WINE WITH SALAD

One of the traditional rules about wine service is that wine should never be served with salad, and probably dates from the time when salad was served as a palate cleanser after the main course. It was typically a very simple salad of greens with a vinaigrette dressing, and the acid of the vinegar was stronger than that in the wine, causing the wines to taste dull and flat.

As we have become more educated about nutrition, salads have become a much more central part of our dining experience. We eat them as a first course or a main course, dressing them with everything from yogurt to peanut sauce. We add small portions of fish, meat, or cheese. We even serve hot entrées on top of salad.

Fortunately, we can now have our salad and drink our wine, too. The secret is simply to make sure that any acid in the dish is less than the acid level of the wine. High-acid wines such as Sauvignon Blanc really shine here, because they allow a higher acid content in the dish.

However, you *can* make a vinaigrette that will work with almost any variety of wine if you keep a proportion of four parts oil to one part vinegar so the dressing will not be too acidic for the wine. In addition, vinegars vary in flavor and acidity just as wines do, so matching vinegars to wine varieties increases the harmony between them. Herbs and spices also have affinities with particular wines. Here are the basics, with some suggested seasonings:

### *Vinaigrette for Sauvignon Blanc*

1 tablespoon white wine vinegar
$1/4$ cup extra-virgin olive oil
salt and freshly ground black pepper to taste
thyme, cilantro, cumin, oregano

### *Vinaigrette for Chardonnay*

1 tablespoon sherry wine vinegar
$1/4$ cup extra-virgin olive oil
salt and freshly ground white pepper to taste
tarragon, chives, curry, ginger, saffron

### Vinaigrette for blush wines

1 tablespoon raspberry vinegar or rice wine vinegar
$^1/_4$ cup vegetable oil
salt and freshly ground black pepper to taste

### Vinaigrette for Pinot Noir

1 tablespoon balsamic vinegar
$^1/_4$ cup extra-virgin olive oil
$^1/_2$ teaspoon soy sauce
freshly ground black pepper to taste

### Vinaigrette for Zinfandel

1 tablespoon balsamic vinegar
$^1/_4$ cup extra-virgin olive oil
salt and freshly ground black pepper to taste
paprika, oregano, basil

### Vinaigrette for Bordeaux varieties

2 teaspoons balsamic vinegar
1 teaspoon white wine vinegar
$^1/_4$ cup extra-virgin olive oil
salt and freshly ground black pepper to taste
rosemary, mustard, savory, thyme

It is definitely worth the money to buy a really good extra-virgin olive oil for use in salad dressings. People are always asking me for the recipe for my vinaigrettes, and I remind them that it is the flavor of the best oil that makes the difference. Notice that I never use red wine vinegar in salad dressings, as it is just too strong, even for red wines.

# WORDS OF CAUTION

## *Artichokes and Wine*

Artichokes do pose a problem for wine because they contain a unique organic acid called cynarin. This acid makes any food or beverage that follows a bite of artichoke taste sweet. The degree of sweetness perceived varies from one person to another because of differences in body chemistry. It is not necessary, however, to give up either artichokes or wine.

You can balance the effect of the cynarin by using a high-acid ingredient such as a very lemony salad dressing in the preparation of the artichoke. Serve it with a Sauvignon Blanc with pronounced acidity. A knowledgeable wine merchant can help you choose a Sauvignon Blanc that is not too fruity in style.

## **The Use of Fruit in Savory Dishes**

Generally, dry wines are preferred as an accompaniment to dining, as they are more refreshing to the palate than sweet wines. As mentioned in the section on sweet textures, the fruit flavors in a dry wine will be overwhelmed by sweetness in a dish, making the wine taste thin, sour, and/or bitter. Therefore, the use of fruit in savory dishes must be very carefully considered when serving a dry wine.

There are several ways to neutralize the sweetness of fruits. The most obvious is to start with those that have lower sugar content, such as blackberries or pomegranates. The sugar can also be neutralized by combining fruit with sour and/or spicy textures, such as is done with fruit salsas. Fruits and dried fruits can also be cooked in a sauce and strained out, leaving the fruit flavors while eliminating the strong hit of sweetness. Finally, cutting fruit in small pieces and cooking in a sauce along with various vegetables will often result in dispersing the fruit sugars throughout the sauce. I always make a point of taste-testing these preparations with the wine I plan to serve to make sure that it works.

# COOKING WITH WINE

Using the same wine that you plan to serve as an ingredient in a dish is a simple way to create a harmonious pairing. Here are a few pointers that you will need to know in order to ensure success when cooking with wine:

## Quality

Most of us would prefer not to use half a bottle of very expensive and/or rare wine for a sauce. It is perfectly acceptable to use a lesser bottle of the same variety that you will be serving, as long as it is a basically sound wine. You might get away with using a flawed wine if it is a small addition to a sauce with lots of other strong flavors, but if you are reducing the wine to concentrate flavors, all the flaws will be concentrated as well.

## Reductions

Besides the caveat to avoid using flawed wines in a reduction, you also need to be aware of the concentration of wine textures that occurs. In dry white wines, the unpleasant concentration of acid can be balanced by the addition of salt to the sauce. Dry red wines will have a concentration of both acid and astringent tannin. Since large amounts of salt can fight with tannin, a subtle sweetening agent is needed. Fruit syrups or liqueurs, maple syrup, or honey will do the trick. Add it judiciously; you don't want the sauce to taste sweet. Black pepper also calms astringency when used in moderate amounts.

## Primary Flavors

Sometimes the flavor of wine in a dish is more subtle than that of other ingredients. White wine, for instance, is traditionally used in the preparation of osso buco, but the cooked tomato flavor in the sauce predominates, calling for a fruity red wine such as Zinfandel.

# Notes About Ingredients

### Produce in Season

All of us who love to cook have repeatedly heard the advice that it is best to use ingredients that are in season. When I began cooking professionally, I realized that I had no idea what *was* in season, since supermarkets now shop the world. In supermarkets, your best clue to seasonality will be price. If you live in an area that has farm markets, it will be time well spent to visit them, making sure to inquire where the farm is located in order to make sure the produce is local and fresh.

Don't expect farm market prices to be lower. Most of these farms are very small, often organic, not cost-effective mass-production operations. What you *can* expect is the discovery that fresh, field-ripened fruits and vegetables have incredible flavors and textures. The better your ingredients, the less you need to do in the kitchen to make a wonderful meal, and the more you work with great produce, the more you will respect it.

### Tomatoes

Once you have found a local farm that grows tomatoes, or begin growing your own, you will find a great many flavors and textures available in the different varieties. If you have meaty tomatoes, such as Romas, use them for making sauces, ketchup, or for pizza toppings. Juicy tomatoes are just the thing for panzanella and other salads in which the juice becomes a part of the acid content of the dressing.

### Green Bell Peppers

I was not surprised when I found that green bell peppers are not a different variety than red. They are simply harvested unripe, and that results in very strong green vegetal flavors. I have not yet found a wine that isn't damaged by these flavors, so I never use them in my cooking.

### Salad Mixes

These combinations of small young lettuces, also sometimes called "mesclun," are becoming more available in markets today. They provide a range of flavors, textures and colors, and have the added advantage of being pre-washed: all you have to do is toss them with a vinaigrette and some seasonings. If you can buy them at a farm market, they will be absolutely fresh, lasting much longer in your refrigerator at home. I also encourage you to *begin* your meal with a salad, when your palate is fresh and best able to enjoy these more subtle foods.

## Fresh Herbs Versus Dried

The flavors of sage, oregano, thyme, and bay become much stronger in their dried form. Parsley, chervil, and chives lose their flavors entirely when dried. No matter which way they go, all the flavors of dried herbs are different than their fresh counterparts, and in most cases, I prefer the flavor of fresh herbs.

Since I don't have the time or conditions to be very successful at gardening, I am delighted that many herbs are very easy to grow. Every year, I stick a few more in the ground outside my kitchen door and gratefully pick whatever survives. I augment these with purchases from farm markets and the growing selection available in supermarkets. If you must use dried herbs, keep in mind that most of their flavor has faded within six months, even when stored in airtight glass jars.

## Nut Oils

Nut oils can add very interesting layers of flavor to vinaigrettes and other cooking. However, I find them to be very prone to rancidity, and recommend buying them in small quantities. Check them immediately for rancidity, and return any to the store that seem bad. Store nut oils in a cool cellar, if you are lucky enough to have one, or in the refrigerator. I use hazelnut oil only in cold dishes, as I have found that just the heat of cooking is enough to make it taste bad.

## Cooking Duck Made Easy

For years I ate duck only at restaurants because I thought it was too difficult to prepare at home. Now I know better. All poultry, in fact, is subject in some degree to the same consideration: each part of the bird requires different cooking methods and time for the best results. The answer is to buy two or three ducks at a time, cut them up, and cook only one part at a time. You can freeze the rest for another meal, since duck has a good layer of fat under the skin to protect it.

Duck breast is best cooked quickly and served medium-rare. Since this does not allow the time necessary to cook out the fat, I remove the skin with the fat first and render it separately. This way, you can have the perfectly cooked meat and the crispy skin, without the unattractive glob of fat.

### Making Fresh Pasta

These days there is so much good dried pasta available, I rarely make it fresh any more. There are two exceptions. The first is spinach pasta, which has a beautiful color and flavor when fresh, and is a travesty of appearance and taste when dried. The other instance in which I make fresh pasta is for ravioli, because I don't care for the puréed fillings of most commercial ravioli. I want something with texture to provide contrast to the smoothness of the noodle. In a pinch, you can use won ton wrappers from the grocery refrigerated case for the pasta, but making your own filling is definitely worth the time.

### Pasta and Pizza Toppings

Over the years, I have reduced the amount of sauce and toppings that I put on pizza and pasta. It is a lighter way of eating that also allows you to enjoy the good grain flavors of the crust and noodles. If you like more "stuff," you may want to increase the quantities called for in these recipes.

### Kosher Salt

Many chefs prefer to use kosher salt rather than the more common iodized table salt. I have read that it is preferable because it enhances flavors with less actual saltiness. I can't prove that, but I do know that it has a coarser grain that is easier to add in pinches, and my fingers have a better sense of quantity without resorting to a measuring spoon. (See *To Taste*, page 27).

### Dried Beans

You may be surprised to learn that dried beans do not last forever. After several experiences with beans that remained hard after long hours of cooking, I realized that it was because they had been languishing in my cupboard for an unknown length of time. If possible, buy beans from a store that shelves them in bulk. The turnover tends to be better, and you don't have to buy more than you need.

When I must buy pre-packed beans, I date the packages and make sure to use them before a year has passed. I am in the "no-pre-soak" camp when it comes to cooking dried beans because I find that pre-soaking dilutes the flavor and often loosens the skins, causing the beans to disintegrate before they are tender. I add salt at the end of the cooking time. The cooked beans seem to have better texture, plus I have the advantage of being able to add salt to my taste.

### Demi-Glace

Demi-glace is called for in several of the recipes in the book. If it is not available in your market, it can be ordered from More Than Gourmet, 1-800-860-9385.

# TO TASTE

Throughout this book you will repeatedly read "salt and freshly ground pepper to taste." If you are fairly new to the kitchen, you may be wondering exactly how much that is. The fact is that tolerance or desire for these very basic flavor-enhancers varies widely from person to person. The best way to determine what you like is to taste, add a little and taste again, until it tastes right to you. In fact, that is what cooking is all about in its entirety.

Once you get familiar with cooking and seasonings, you will find yourself measuring less and less, and tasting more. Your fingers will begin to know automatically how big a pinch to use. This is when cooking really starts to be fun, rather than a strict regimen of following directions and rules. And the more you taste, the more you will realize the intelligence of your own palate.

S A U V I G N

Sauvignon Blanc is a wonderful, dry white wine. Its fresh, crisp style makes it one of the most "food friendly" wines being made, yet thirty years ago almost no one in the United States would try it. Robert Mondavi, acknowledged genius of the California wine industry, came up with the idea of calling it Fumé Blanc, borrowing the Fumé from the then more well known Pouilly-Fumé, a French Sauvignon Blanc from the Loire region. This idea worked so well that many wineries today still use that name, while others have chosen to stick with the varietal name, Sauvignon Blanc. Whatever the name, the grape is the same.

Sauvignon Blanc is traditionally made in a lighter, high-acid style, which can easily match the acid in a vinaigrette dressing, so we can throw out that old adage about never serving wine with salad. High acidity also creates a good balance with salty foods and green vegetables, as is obvious in a quick perusal of the food profile.

O N B L A N C

## CHAMELEON RECIPES

## SAUVIGNON BLANC RECIPES

# SAUVIGNON BLANC PROFILE

## Food Affinities

| SEAFOOD | MEAT & POULTRY | HERBS & SPICES | SAUCES | CHEESE & NUTS | VEGETABLES & FRUITS |
|---------|----------------|----------------|--------|---------------|---------------------|
| anchovies | chicken | black pepper | citrus | feta cheese | artichokes |
| crab | prosciutto | capers | vinaigrettes | fresh goat | asparagus |
| raw clams | | chives | yogurt | cheese | cucumbers |
| raw oysters | | cilantro | | Parmesan | eggplant |
| scallops | | cumin | | cheese | fresh tomatoes |
| shrimp | | garlic | | | green beans |
| smoked fish | | oregano | | | kalamata olives |
| trout | | thyme | | | lemon |
| tuna | | | | | lettuces |
| | | | | | lime |
| | | | | | raw bell |
| | | | | | peppers |
| | | | | | raw corn |
| | | | | | snow peas |
| | | | | | zucchini |

## Food Conflicts

| SEAFOOD | MEAT & POULTRY | HERBS & SPICES | SAUCES | CHEESE & NUTS | VEGETABLES & FRUITS |
|---------|----------------|----------------|--------|---------------|---------------------|
| lobster | bacon | cinnamon | butter | blue cheese | avocado |
| sturgeon | foie gras | cloves | cream | Brie cheese | mashed potato |
| | red meats | curry | soy | Swiss cheese | pumpkin |
| | sausage | ginger | | walnuts | sweet potato |

### Wine Flavors:
New-mown hay, fresh-cut grass, grapefruit, fig, green herbs, bell pepper

### Wine Textures:
Acid

### Complementary Cuisines:
Mediterranean, vegetarian, California

### Best Methods of Preparation:
Grilling, smoking, sautéing in oil; uncooked foods, such as salads, crudités, and raw fish

### Best Seasons:
Serve Sauvignon Blanc in the spring and summer, when the weather gets warmer and gardens start producing bumper crops of fresh herbs and vegetables.

### Ideal Occasions:
The lighter style of Sauvignon Blanc is particularly enjoyable at luncheons, crabfests, or a Friday night grill with chicken or fish.

Sweet red peppers are wine-friendly and can be enjoyed with a wide variety of wines, depending on their preparation. This recipe takes the peppers to Sauvignon Blanc with the green herb flavor of thyme and the tanginess provided by the yogurt. Using nonfat stock and nonfat yogurt can also keep the soup lighter in body, matching the body of the wine.

Serves Six to Eight

This soup can also be made into a match for Chardonnay by substituting fennel seed for the thyme and heavy cream for the yogurt.

# RED PEPPER SOUP

6 red bell peppers, seeded, chopped
1 cup chopped onion
1 small clove garlic, minced
1 teaspoon dried thyme
1 bay leaf
3 tablespoons olive oil
$1/4$ cup flour
4 cups nonfat chicken stock or vegetable stock
2 fresh tomatoes, peeled, seeded, chopped
1 tablespoon tomato paste
$1/2$ cup nonfat yogurt
salt and freshly ground black pepper to taste
nonfat yogurt and fresh thyme leaves for garnish

1. Sauté the bell peppers, onion, garlic, thyme and bay leaf in the heated olive oil in a heavy-bottomed saucepan over medium heat until the vegetables are tender.

2. Stir in the flour. Cook over low heat for 10 minutes, stirring constantly. Add the stock, tomatoes and tomato paste and mix well. Simmer over medium heat for 45 minutes.

3. Purée in a blender or food processor. Combine with $1/2$ cup yogurt in the saucepan. Simmer for 10 minutes. Season with salt and black pepper. Ladle into soup bowls. Garnish with a dollop of additional yogurt and a fresh thyme leaf.

Note: The red peppers should be a vibrant red for the most colorful presentation.

# RISI E BISI

1 medium onion, chopped
3 tablespoons unsalted butter
2 slices prosciutto, diced
4 cups fresh chicken broth or canned low-salt chicken broth
1 cup Sauvignon Blanc
1 cup uncooked Arborio rice
2 cups small green peas
salt and freshly ground black pepper to taste
¾ cup freshly grated Asiago or Parmesan cheese and
2 tablespoons minced Italian parsley for garnish

1. Sauté the onion in the butter in a large saucepan until tender. Add the prosciutto and cook for 2 minutes longer.

2. Add the chicken stock and wine. Bring to a boil. Stir in the rice gradually and reduce the heat. Simmer until the rice is almost tender.

3. Add the peas. Return to a simmer and cook for 3 minutes or just until the rice and peas are tender. Season with salt and pepper. Ladle into soup bowls and garnish with cheese and parsley.

*The butter and chicken stock in this traditional Italian rice and pea soup would suggest a Chardonnay, but it is actually better suited to Sauvignon Blanc. The key is matching the intensity of the soup and the wine. The body of the soup is very light and further refreshed by the barely cooked peas and fresh Italian parsley. A typical Chardonnay appears overly heavy by comparison, and the hint of saltiness from the prosciutto and the cheese is better balanced by the acidic style of Sauvignon Blanc.*

Serves Four to Six

Corn is on the food affinities lists for both Chardonnay and Sauvignon Blanc. Just cut off the cob and served uncooked, it has the fresh flavor that best complements Sauvignon Blanc, as its sweetness contrasts with the acids in the wine. The acids of the vinaigrette and the slight saltiness of the grated cheese pull the dish together, a great interplay of flavors and textures.

Serves Six

# ARUGULA SALAD WITH CORN AND RED PEPPER

1 red bell pepper
2 fresh ears corn
6 ounces tender arugula leaves
3 tablespoons white wine vinaigrette
1 to 2 ounces freshly grated Parmesan or Asiago cheese
freshly ground black pepper to taste

1. Seed the bell pepper, discarding white membranes; cut into fine julienne slices. Cut the corn from the cobs.

2. Combine the bell pepper, corn, arugula and vinaigrette. Divide among salad plates. Top with cheese and pepper.

# GARDEN SALAD WITH GOAT CHEESE AND SUN GOLD TOMATOES

¾ cup dried beans such as lima beans, navy beans, flageolets,
cranberry beans, pinto beans, kidney beans, or black beans
salt to taste
1 tablespoon white wine vinegar
¼ cup extra-virgin olive oil
freshly ground black pepper to taste
8 ounces haricots verts or green beans
8 ounces Sun Gold cherry tomatoes
4 ounces fresh goat cheese, sliced
2 teaspoons fresh thyme leaves

1. Select 2 or 3 of the varieties of dried beans. Rinse and sort the beans. Combine each variety with water to cover in a separate saucepan. Cook for about 1 hour or just until tender. Drain the beans and combine with salt in a bowl, tossing gently to mix well.

2. For the vinaigrette, combine the wine vinegar and olive oil with salt and pepper to taste in a bowl and whisk until smooth. Spoon some of the vinaigrette into the bean mixture and mix gently.

3. Cut large green beans into halves lengthwise and crosswise. Blanch in boiling salted water for 1 to 3 minutes or just until tender-crisp. Drain and plunge into ice water to stop the cooking process; drain again. Add to the salad.

4. Cut the tomatoes into halves. Add to the salad. Correct the seasoning and toss to mix well.

5. Spoon onto salad plates. Top with a slice of cheese. Drizzle with the remaining vinaigrette and sprinkle with the thyme leaves.

*Sun Gold tomatoes are orange cherry tomatoes with an intense sweet flavor. Local farm markets are the best sources for them, but if Sun Golds are not available, any ripe cherry tomato in season will work. This salad, packed with the fresh flavors of green beans, green herbs and tangy goat cheese, is best complemented by a fresh-tasting Sauvignon Blanc. The acidity of the wine can easily handle the acids of the tomatoes and vinaigrette.*

Serves Four to Six

# ORZO AND SPINACH SALAD

12 ounces uncooked orzo (Greek rice-shaped pasta)
2 tablespoons olive oil
2 teaspoons lemon juice
1/2 cup olive oil
3 tablespoons white wine vinegar
1 teaspoon Dijon mustard
1 small clove garlic, minced
1/8 teaspoon dried thyme
1/2 teaspoon dried oregano
1/4 teaspoon ground cumin
salt and freshly ground black pepper to taste
2 bunches spinach, torn into bite-size pieces
1/2 cup slivered kalamata olives
1 red bell pepper, julienned
2 green onions, minced (dark green and white portions)
1 tablespoon capers, rinsed, drained
2 ounces feta cheese, crumbled

1. Cook the orzo al dente using the package directions. Drain, rinse with cold water and drain well. Combine with 2 tablespoons olive oil in a large bowl and toss to coat.

2. For the dressing, combine the lemon juice with 1/2 cup olive oil, wine vinegar, Dijon mustard, garlic, thyme, oregano, cumin, salt and pepper in a bowl and mix well. Add to the orzo.

3. Add the spinach, olives, bell pepper, green onions and capers and toss to mix well.* Add the cheese to the salad and toss gently. Correct the seasoning. Divide among 8 salad plates.

*The salad may be held in the refrigerator for several hours at this point.

Note: The addition of 12 ounces of cooked bay shrimp makes this into a very nice entrée salad.

# STUFFED TOMATOES WITH CORN AND FRESH GOAT CHEESE

4 (4-ounce) vine-ripened tomatoes
1 ear fresh sweet corn
1 shallot, finely minced
3 ounces fresh goat cheese, crumbled
4 ounces cherry tomatoes, diced*
1 teaspoon fresh thyme leaves
salt and freshly ground black pepper to taste
thyme oil
cherry tomato halves and thyme sprigs for garnish

1. Cut the tops off the large tomatoes and discard. Scoop out the seeds and pulp with a melon baller or spoon, reserving the shells.

2. For the filling, cut the corn from the cob. Combine the corn with the shallot and cheese in a small bowl. Add the cherry tomatoes and thyme leaves and mix gently with a fork. Season with salt and pepper.

3. Spoon the filling into the tomato shells, mounding the tops. Serve on salad plates glossed with thyme oil and garnish with additional cherry tomatoes and thyme sprigs.

*Use a combination of red, orange and yellow cherry tomatoes if available.

*The acids in fresh tomatoes achieve the best balance on the palate with high-acid Sauvignon Blanc, although the other ingredients and the method of preparation of a dish are also important. Here, the fresh vegetables and herbs echo the freshness of the wine and, even though fresh goat cheese has some creamy fat content, it also has a definite acid tang which predominates. It could be lightened up further, if desired, by surrounding the tomatoes with some small lettuce leaves tossed with a little white wine vinaigrette.*

Serves Four

All of the ingredients for this dish
are fresh and light, as is a classic
Sauvignon Blanc. The acid of the lime
juice is in balance with that of the wine,
and the snow peas and yellow peppers
provide the fresh vegetable complement.
If tobiko caviar, the roe of the flying
fish, is available, it gives a nice
touch of contrast with its salt and
crunchy texture, but it is unnecessary
for the success of the dish.

Serves Six

# LIME-MARINATED SCALLOP SALAD

1 1/4 pounds fresh bay scallops
juice of 3 limes
1 shallot, minced
salt and freshly ground black pepper to taste
2 yellow bell peppers, seeded, chopped
1/2 small yellow onion, chopped
1 clove garlic, minced
1 tablespoon olive oil
1 tablespoon white wine vinegar
1 tablespoon fresh lime juice
salt to taste
1/3 pound snow peas
tobiko caviar or diced red bell pepper for garnish

1. To marinate the scallops,
rinse them and pat dry, removing any attached muscles. Combine
with the juice of 3 limes, shallot, salt and pepper in a noncorrosive
bowl. Marinate, covered, in the refrigerator for 2 hours or until the
scallops have become opaque and "cooked" by the action of the
acid in the lime juice.

2. Combine the bell peppers,
onion, garlic, olive oil, wine vinegar and 1 tablespoon lime juice in a
small noncorrosive saucepan. Simmer, covered, for 30 minutes or
until the bell peppers are tender, adding water during the cooking
time if necessary to prevent browning. Cool to room temperature.
Purée in a blender or food processor; press through a strainer. Season
to taste with salt.

3. Blanch the snow peas in
boiling water; refresh in ice water and drain well. Cut into fine
julienne strips.

4. Mound the scallops in
the centers of 6 salad plates. Spoon the pepper sauce and snow
peas around the scallops. Garnish the scallops with the caviar or
bell pepper.

# ROCK SHRIMP REMOULADE WITH GRILLED ASPARAGUS

2 cornichons, minced
2 teaspoons capers, rinsed, drained
1 tablespoon chopped Italian parsley
1 tablespoon chopped chives
1 teaspoon Dijon mustard
1/4 cup mayonnaise, low-fat mayonnaise or nonfat mayonnaise
1/4 cup sour cream, low-fat sour cream or nonfat sour cream
1 pound cooked peeled rock shrimp or bay shrimp
24 asparagus spears
1 tablespoon olive oil
salt and freshly ground black pepper to taste
chives for garnish

1. For the remoulade sauce, combine the cornichons, capers, parsley, 1 tablespoon chives, Dijon mustard, mayonnaise and sour cream in a medium bowl.

2. Rinse the shrimp and pat dry. Add to the remoulade sauce and mix well. Chill, covered, in the refrigerator.*

3. Trim the asparagus spears to the same length. Combine with the olive oil, salt and pepper in a shallow dish, coating well.

4. Preheat a gas grill or prepare a charcoal fire. Grill the asparagus for 2 to 3 minutes or just until the spears begin to turn color.

5. Spoon the shrimp mixture onto the centers of serving plates. Arrange the asparagus around the shrimp. Garnish with chives and serve immediately.

*Shrimp remoulade may be made a day in advance and chilled for up to 24 hours.

Note: When asparagus is out of season, substitute about 10 to 12 blanched haricots verts per serving and toss with a small amount of vinaigrette.

*I've never understood why asparagus was on that list of food-with-wine no-no's handed down through the years. Its fresh green vegetable flavor is perfectly complemented by a fresh acidic Sauvignon Blanc. To make the classic French remoulade more appropriate, I have omitted the tarragon with its sweet notes, and cut the richness of mayonnaise by using part sour cream.*

Serves Six as a First Course
or
Four as an Entrée

*This is a contemporary version of
the traditional Italian Pasta alla
Puttanesca. The use of fresh rather than
canned tomatoes lightens the dish
considerably. The acids in the fresh
tomatoes and capers with the saltiness
of the anchovies and olives provide
the perfect balance with the acids
in a Sauvignon Blanc.*

Serves Four

# SPAGHETTINI WITH TOMATOES AND OLIVES

2 pounds ripe fresh tomatoes
12 ounces uncooked spaghettini
¼ cup olive oil
8 anchovy fillets, coarsely chopped
1 tablespoon minced garlic
2 tablespoons capers, rinsed, drained
20 pitted kalamata olives, sliced
freshly ground black pepper to taste
2 tablespoons coarsely chopped Italian parsley for garnish

1. Immerse the tomatoes in boiling water for 1 minute or just until the skins loosen. Drain and remove the skins. Cut the tomatoes into halves horizontally and squeeze out the seeds. Cut into medium dice and set aside.

2. Combine the spaghettini with boiling salted water in a large saucepan and begin cooking.

3. Heat the olive oil in a sauté pan. Add the anchovies and cook until they begin to disintegrate. Add the garlic. Cook for 1 minute, stirring constantly; do not brown. Add the tomatoes, capers and olives. Cook until heated through.

4. Drain the cooked pasta well. Combine with the sauce in a pasta bowl and add pepper; toss to mix well. Serve immediately, garnished with parsley.

# Pasta with Smoked Oysters

1 pound uncooked linguine
1 teaspoon salt
1/2 large red onion, chopped
1/2 red bell pepper, seeded, cut into strips
1/2 yellow bell pepper, seeded, cut into strips
2 tablespoons olive oil
1/2 cup pitted kalamata olives
1 small can smoked oysters, drained
1 bunch spinach, washed, stemmed, coarsely chopped
salt and freshly ground black pepper to taste
4 ounces crumbled feta cheese for garnish

1. Cook the linguine al dente with 1 teaspoon salt in boiling water in a large saucepan.

2. While the pasta is cooking, sauté the onion and bell peppers in the olive oil in a sauté pan over medium-low heat until tender-crisp. Add the olives, oysters and spinach. Cook just until the spinach begins to wilt.

3. Drain the pasta and combine with the oyster mixture in a pasta bowl. Add salt and pepper to taste and toss gently to mix well. Serve immediately, garnished with feta cheese.

*Sauvignon Blanc goes best with this combination of fresh vegetables and salty foods. The acids in the wine balance the salt, refresh the palate, and match the fresh flavors of the vegetables.*

Serves Four

The freshness and acidity of a
Sauvignon Blanc are requisites for
the enjoyment of the saltiness of the
anchovies on this pizza. Cooking the
onions in advance and using frozen puff
pastry make it very fast to assemble. It
is equally delicious hot or just slightly
warm and can be cut into small pieces
for a great hors d'oeuvre.

Serves Six

A high-acid blush wine also works
well with this recipe.

# PIZZA NIÇOISE ON PUFF PASTRY

4 medium onions, thinly sliced
2 tablespoons olive oil
1 teaspoon fresh thyme leaves or ½ teaspoon dried thyme
1 tablespoon chopped Italian parsley
salt and freshly ground black pepper to taste
1 sheet frozen puff pastry, thawed
¼ cup grated Asiago or Parmesan cheese
6 anchovy fillets
12 pitted niçoise olives

**1.** Cook the onions in the olive oil
in a saucepan over low heat for 30 minutes or until tender. Stir in the
thyme, parsley, salt and pepper.

**2.** Preheat the oven to 400
degrees. Line a baking sheet with baking parchment. Place the
pastry on the prepared baking sheet and prick with a fork. Fold up
the edges and crimp.

**3.** Spread the onions over the
pastry and sprinkle with the cheese. Arrange the anchovies in a
decorative pattern over the top. Bake for 30 to 40 minutes or until the
pastry is light brown. Sprinkle with the olives. Cut into pieces to serve.

# CRAB CAKES

½ small onion, minced
1 tablespoon unsalted butter
½ cup soft bread crumbs
2 tablespoons heavy cream
2 eggs
3 tablespoons minced parsley
1 tablespoon minced chives
½ teaspoon dry mustard
⅛ teaspoon Tabasco sauce
cayenne pepper to taste
½ teaspoon salt
2 cups crab meat, about 14 ounces
1 cup dry bread crumbs
vegetable oil for frying

1. Sauté the onion in the butter in a sauté pan for 3 minutes or until tender.

2. Soak the soft bread crumbs in the cream in a medium bowl. Beat the eggs in a bowl until frothy. Add to the bread crumb mixture.

3. Add the onion mixture, parsley, chives, dry mustard, Tabasco sauce, cayenne pepper and salt and mix well. Fold in the crab meat. Shape into 8 cakes and dust with the dry bread crumbs.

4. Fry in the vegetable oil in a skillet over medium heat until golden brown on both sides. Serve immediately.

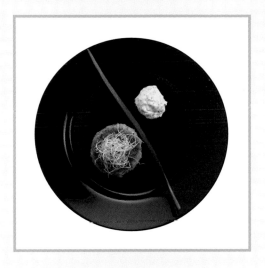

*Is there anyone who doesn't love crab cakes except those unfortunate people who have allergies to seafood? This version has the added advantage of being quite wine-friendly. Serve it with a remoulade sauce (page 39) for a delightful treat with Sauvignon Blanc.*

Serves Four

*The rich, fattier flavors and textures of a sweet red pepper aïoli swing this dish over to Chardonnay.*

*These tostadas have a fresh and lively texture and flavor that are perfectly matched by a fresh and lively Sauvignon Blanc; its herbal aspects can even handle the pungency of cilantro. The tang of the fresh goat cheese aligns with the acid in the wine, while the saltiness of the smoked salmon creates balance.*

Serves Six
——————

# SMOKED SALMON TOSTADAS

1 cup dried small white beans*
1 fresh jalapeño, cut into halves, seeded*
1 (2-inch) cube salt pork (optional)*
4 ounces fresh goat cheese
salt to taste
1/2 red bell pepper, chopped
1/2 yellow bell pepper, chopped
1/2 red onion, chopped
olive oil
rice wine vinegar
corn oil for frying
12 small white corn tortillas
leaves of 1 bunch cilantro
4 ounces smoked salmon, thinly sliced
1 cup light sour cream

1. Rinse and sort the white beans. Combine with the jalapeño and salt pork in a saucepan. Cook for 1 1/2 hours or until the beans are very tender; drain.

2. Combine with the cheese in a food processor container and process until smooth. Season with salt and set aside.

3. For the pepper relish, combine the bell peppers and onion in a medium bowl. Add just enough olive oil and vinegar to moisten and mix well.

4. Heat 1 inch of corn oil in a heavy iron skillet. Add the tortillas 1 at a time and fry just until they begin to color. Drain well on paper towels.

5. Spread the bean purée on the tortillas. Top with cilantro and a slice of smoked salmon. Spoon a dollop of sour cream on each tostada and top with the pepper relish.

*To simplify preparation, use drained canned beans, such as Trappey brand, packed with salt pork and jalapeños.

Note: For hors d'oeuvre presentation, cut small circles from the tortillas with a cookie cutter before frying and adjust the size of the toppings. Omit the pepper relish.

# SALMON TARTARE

1 1/2 pounds fresh salmon
3 tablespoons fresh lemon juice
1/2 cup chopped Italian parsley
1/2 cup chopped chives
6 tablespoons minced shallots
1/4 cup minced cornichons
1/4 cup capers, rinsed, drained
3 tablespoons prepared horseradish
3 tablespoons Dijon mustard
8 drops Tabasco sauce
salt to taste
cucumber slices and chives for garnish

1. Discard the skin and bones from the salmon and chop very fine. Combine with the lemon juice, parsley, 1/2 cup chives, shallots, cornichons, capers, horseradish, Dijon mustard, Tabasco sauce and salt in a bowl and mix well.

2. Chill for 1 hour or longer; the longer the mixture sits, the more the lemon juice will "cook" the salmon. Serve chilled, garnished with cucumber and chives.

*Salmon have a high fat content and rich flavor, which usually call for a full-bodied wine like Chardonnay. The lemon juice used to "cook" the salmon, in addition to the acid of the capers and cornichons, would make a Chardonnay seem heavy and clumsy in this dish, and a high-acid Sauvignon is needed to balance the acidity.*

Serves Eight

Most shellfish are equally enjoyable with Sauvignon Blanc or Chardonnay. The deciding factors in the choice of wine will be the method of preparation and the other ingredients in the dish. Grilling scallops with a brush of olive oil allows the clear sweet flavor to make a delicate balance with a crisp Sauvignon Blanc. The addition of the sweet pepper relish provides a fresh complement to the wine.

Serves Six

# GRILLED SCALLOPS WITH SWEET PEPPER RELISH

1½ pounds fresh ocean scallops
olive oil
salt and freshly ground black pepper to taste
2 bell peppers, any color but green
½ red onion
white wine or rice wine vinegar
chives for garnish

1. Remove the tough membranes from the scallops and pat dry. Combine with just enough olive oil to coat well in a bowl and toss lightly; season with salt and pepper.

2. For the relish, discard the stem, seeds and membranes of the bell peppers. Cut the peppers and onion into ⅛-inch dice. Sprinkle with the vinegar in a bowl; season with salt and pepper.

3. Preheat a gas grill or prepare a charcoal fire. Grill the scallops for 3 minutes or until cooked through, turning when the edges begin to turn opaque.

4. Spoon the scallops onto 6 warmed plates. Top with the pepper relish and garnish with chives.

Note: For hors d'oeuvre servings, place one scallop and a small amount of relish in a small lettuce cup.

# SMOKED TROUT MOUSSE WITH BELGIAN ENDIVE

12 ounces smoked trout, skinned, boned
⅓ cup sour cream or nonfat sour cream
2 tablespoons lemon juice
1 tablespoon prepared horseradish, or to taste
3 or 4 Belgian endive
chives and chive oil for garnish

1. Cut about 4 ounces of the trout into small squares or triangles. Cover and reserve in the refrigerator.

2. For the mousse, combine the remaining trout with the sour cream, lemon juice and horseradish in a food processor container. Process for 10 to 15 seconds or until smooth. Spoon into a small container. Chill, covered, for 1 hour or longer.

3. Separate the endive into leaves. Spoon the trout mixture into the center of 8 serving plates. Arrange the endive leaves around the trout in a flower design. Arrange the reserved trout between the endive leaves. Sprinkle with the chives and drizzle the chive oil on the plate.

*Smoked fish go well with Sauvignon Blanc because their salt content is best balanced with a high-acid wine. The high-acid styles of Champagne are also good choices, albeit more expensive. The lemon juice and horseradish in this recipe provide some zippy spice and bite, which also call for the brightness of Sauvignon Blanc.*

Serves Six to Eight

*This recipe definitely argues with the old rule of thumb about serving red wine with meat. In this case, the strong green herb flavors of the cilantro and cumin supersede the red meat flavors of the lamb, making Sauvignon Blanc the wine of choice.*

Serves Four

# Lamb with Cilantro and Cumin Crust

2 whole lamb loins, with or without tenderloins
olive oil
salt to taste
leaves of ½ bunch cilantro
2 tablespoons ground cumin
½ teaspoon cayenne pepper

1. Clean the lamb of all fat and silver skin. Brush with olive oil and sprinkle with salt.

2. Process the cilantro with the cumin and cayenne pepper in a food processor. Add enough olive oil 1 tablespoon at a time to make a mixture the consistency of jam, processing constantly.

3. Spread the cilantro mixture over the lamb. Let stand at room temperature for 30 to 60 minutes or in the refrigerator for 8 hours or longer.

4. Preheat a gas grill or prepare a charcoal fire. Grill the lamb for 4 minutes on each side for rare or until done to taste when tested with the point of a sharp knife. Let stand for several minutes. Slice and arrange on a warmed plate.

# CHICKEN CHARMOULA

1 clove garlic
2 tablespoons chopped flat-leaf Italian parsley
2 tablespoons chopped cilantro
1 tablespoon ground cumin
1 tablespoon sweet paprika
1 teaspoon salt
1/2 teaspoon cayenne pepper
1/4 cup lemon juice
1/4 cup olive oil
6 boneless skinless chicken breast halves
1 cup nonfat yogurt
cilantro sprigs for garnish

1. For the seasoning mixture, mince the garlic in a food processor fitted with a steel blade to make about 1 teaspoon minced garlic. Add the parsley, cilantro, cumin, paprika, salt and cayenne pepper and process until minced. Add the lemon juice and olive oil and process until smooth.

2. Rinse the chicken and pat dry. Spread half the seasoning mixture over the chicken and cover. Chill the chicken and remaining seasoning mixture for 2 to 12 hours.

3. Preheat the broiler or prepare a fire in the grill. Grill or broil the chicken for 3 minutes on each side or until it springs back to the touch and is cooked through. Place on serving plates.

4. Mix the reserved seasoning mixture with the yogurt. Serve the chicken with a dollop of the yogurt sauce and grilled vegetables chosen from the profile chart; garnish with the cilantro.

Note: This dish is equally good hot or at room temperature. It also makes great sandwiches.

This recipe was inspired by a traditional Moroccan seasoning. The strong green herbs, the heat from the cayenne pepper, and the acid of the lemon juice would fight with any wine other than Sauvignon Blanc. Ask your local wine merchant to help you avoid the softer "wanna-be-Chardonnay" styles of this varietal, however, which would not work nearly as well with this dish.

Serves Six

C H A R D

Chardonnay is the most popular wine varietal in the world. The classic grape of White Burgundy and Chablis, and the star of the California roster, varietally named Chardonnay is now being produced in Australia and New Zealand, South America, South Africa, Italy, all over the United States, and even in other regions of France. As well as being consumed in great quantity as a still wine, it is also used extensively in making fine Champagne and sparkling wines.

Chardonnay is loved by growers, for it is relatively easy to grow. It is loved by winemakers, as it is a very versatile grape that can display many possible flavors and textures on the palate, depending on how they practice their art in the cellar. It is loved by consumers for its forward fruit flavors that can range from lemon and green apple all the way to lush tropical fruits such as pineapple and banana. The variety also works well with fermentation in oak, which produces a rich buttery character, and oak aging, which adds vanilla. If you don't have access to wine tastings, you must rely on wine journalists or the staff of fine wine shops to identify the styles of various producers.

The same things that make Chardonnay the darling of growers and winemakers can be a stumbling block for a chef. Although there is a long list of foods that go well with the wine, a chef must keep a dish for Chardonnay fairly simple. A dish with complex flavors will fight for attention with the many flavors in the wine, leaving the palate, and the diner, exhausted.

O          N          N          A          Y

## CHAMELEON RECIPES

## CHARDONNAY RECIPES

# CHARDONNAY PROFILE

## Food Affinities

| SEAFOOD | MEAT & POULTRY | HERBS & SPICES | SAUCES | CHEESE & NUTS | VEGETABLES & FRUITS |
|---|---|---|---|---|---|
| cooked oysters | bacon | basil | butter | Asiago cheese | avocado |
| lobster | chicken | chervil | cream | fontina cheese | chanterelles |
| monkfish | pheasant | chives | hazelnut oil | Jack cheese | cooked sweet |
| mussels | pork | fennel seed | mayonnaise | mozzarella | peppers |
| salmon | quail | fresh sage | velouté | cheese | corn/polenta |
| sea bass | rabbit | garlic | | hazelnuts | fennel |
| scallops | sweetbreads | mild curry | | pecans | green cabbage |
| shark | turkey breast | mild ginger | | pumpkin seeds | green olives |
| shrimp | veal | mustard | | sesame seeds | porcini |
| sturgeon | | nutmeg | | | potato |
| swordfish | | saffron | | | pumpkin |
| | | tarragon | | | shiitake |
| | | white pepper | | | spinach |
| | | | | | squash |
| | | | | | white beans |

## Food Conflicts

| SEAFOOD | MEAT & POULTRY | HERBS & SPICES | SAUCES | CHEESE & NUTS | VEGETABLES & FRUITS |
|---|---|---|---|---|---|
| anchovies | beef | cilantro | barbecue | blue cheese | artichokes |
| mackerel | lamb | cinnamon | lime | Camembert | asparagus |
| sole | squab | dill | salsa | cheese | green beans |
| tuna | | rosemary | | | most fruit |

**Wine Flavors:**
Full-flavored, rich; lemon, apple, pineapple, banana, cooked apple, coconut, vanilla, butter, honey

**Wine Textures:**
Fruit, acid, fat

**Complementary Cuisines:**
French, North Italian, and American dishes tend to combine well with Chardonnay.

**Best Methods of Preparation:**
Roasting, sautéing in butter, grilling

**Best Seasons:**
Fall and winter are great times to enjoy this rich, complex wine.

**Ideal Occasions:**
Formal dinners really show Chardonnay at its best.

Anytime butter, cream, and cheese appear in a recipe, it is almost certain to be best enjoyed with Chardonnay, preferably a big fat one. Asiago cheese, although similar to Parmesan, has a sweet aspect that echoes the fruity flavors in the wine. Using the same wine as part of the soup base confirms the match.

Serves Six to Eight

# ASIAGO CREAM SOUP WITH CAPPELLINI

½ cup unsalted butter
1 cup freshly grated Asiago cheese
3 egg yolks
1 cup heavy cream
1 cup Chardonnay
4 cups chicken stock
4 ounces uncooked cappellini or fideos
salt and freshly ground white pepper to taste
chopped parsley or chives for garnish

1. Cream the butter in a food processor. Add the cheese and process for 2 minutes. Add the egg yolks 1 at a time, processing briefly after each addition.

2. Add the cream with the food processor running; scrape down the side of the container and process again; set aside.

3. Bring the wine and chicken stock to a boil in a saucepan. Break the pasta into the saucepan. Cook for 8 minutes or until al dente.

4. Spoon some of the hot soup into the mixture in the food processor and process until smooth. Add to the saucepan. Bring to a simmer and season with salt and white pepper. Ladle into soup bowls; garnish with parsley or chives.

# Roasted Onion and Garlic Bisque

10 stems parsley
5 fresh sage leaves
1 bay leaf
2 large heads garlic
2 pounds assorted allium such as white onions,
yellow onions, leek bulbs and shallots
2 medium carrots
2 tablespoons olive oil
2 tablespoons melted butter
6 cups chicken stock or vegetable stock, or 2 small cans stock
and 2 cups water
1/2 loaf stale French bread, crumbled
2 cups half-and-half
salt and freshly ground white pepper to taste
8 toasted baguette rounds and 1 package onion sprouts or
2 tablespoons chopped chives for garnish

1. Preheat the oven to 350 degrees. Tie the parsley, sage and bay leaf into a bouquet garni.

2. Separate the garlic heads into cloves and mash the cloves with the side of a large knife or cleaver. Peel and coarsely chop the allium and carrots. Combine the allium and carrots with the garlic in a roasting pan and drizzle with the olive oil and butter.

3. Roast for 1 1/2 hours or until the garlic is very tender and the other vegetables are tender and beginning to brown. Discard the garlic skins.

4. Combine the vegetables with the chicken stock, bouquet garni and bread in a saucepan. Simmer for 15 to 20 minutes. Discard the bouquet garni.

5. Purée the soup in several batches in a food processor. Press through a strainer into the saucepan. Add the half-and-half, salt and white pepper. Heat just to serving temperature. Ladle into soup bowls. Serve with baguette slices topped with onion sprouts or chives.

*This soup has very rich deep flavors which happily derive more from the slow roasting of the vegetables than the addition of butter or cream. It works well with a big intensely-flavored Chardonnay. Like a good Chardonnay, it improves with age, so make it a day or two before you plan to serve it, for maximum enjoyment.*

Serves Eight

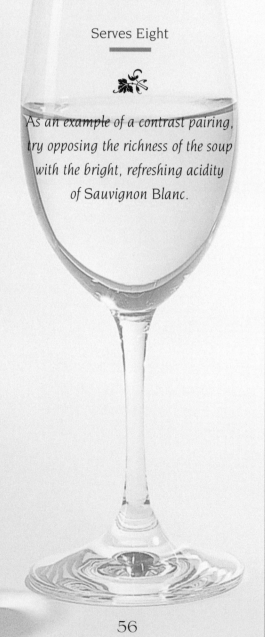

*Corn can be enjoyed with almost any white wine, with the method of preparation defining the wine choice. Here the corn is roasted with butter, tying into the buttery toasty flavors of a good Chardonnay. The addition of cream also matches the soup to the creamy texture of Chardonnay.*

Serves Eight

*As an example of a contrast pairing, try opposing the richness of the soup with the bright, refreshing acidity of Sauvignon Blanc.*

# ROASTED SWEET CORN SOUP

10 to 12 ears fresh corn in the husks
¼ cup unsalted butter
4 large cloves garlic
4 cups homemade or canned low-salt chicken stock
2 cups water
1 large baking potato, peeled, cut into eighths
4 teaspoons cornmeal
1 cup heavy cream
salt and black pepper to taste
basil oil and basil sprigs for garnish

1. Preheat the oven to 450 degrees. Pull away some of the corn husks, leaving the base intact. Place some of the butter on each ear and replace the husks. Place in a baking pan with the garlic cloves.

2. Roast for 20 minutes. Cool to room temperature. Peel the garlic and shuck the corn. Scrape the kernels from the corn, reserving 2 cups of the corn and 6 corn cobs.

3. Combine the chicken stock and water in a saucepan. Add the corn cobs, garlic and potato. Simmer until the potato is tender. Discard the corn cobs.

4. Process the stock mixture, remaining corn kernels and cornmeal in several batches in a food processor until puréed. Combine with the cream in the saucepan. Bring just to a boil. Stir in the reserved corn kernels, salt and pepper. Ladle into soup bowls and serve immediately. Garnish with basil oil and basil sprigs.

# ROCK SHRIMP SALAD WITH FRESH CORN AND POTATOES

clarified butter
2 large baking potatoes
salt to taste
2 pounds boiling potatoes, such as Yukon Gold or Yellow Finn
1¼ pounds cooked rock shrimp
1 cup corn freshly cut from the cob
1 cup mayonnaise
1 cup sour cream*
2 tablespoons chopped fresh chervil
2 tablespoons chopped chives
freshly ground white pepper to taste
chives and chervil leaves for garnish

1. Preheat the oven to 400 degrees. Line a baking sheet with parchment and brush it with clarified butter.

2. For the potato crisps, peel the baking potatoes and slice very thinly lengthwise. Arrange the slices on the prepared baking sheet. Brush with the butter and season lightly with salt. Cover with another sheet of parchment and top with a fine-screen baking rack.

3. Bake the slices for 15 minutes, Check for doneness, rearranging as necessary for even browning. Bake until golden brown. Drain and cool on paper towels.

4. For the salad, cook the boiling potatoes in salted boiling water in a saucepan just until tender; drain. Let stand until cool enough to handle. Peel and cut into ½-inch dice.

5. Combine the diced potatoes with the shrimp, corn, mayonnaise, sour cream, chervil and 2 tablespoons chives in a bowl and mix gently. Season with salt and white pepper to taste.

6. Mound the salad in the centers of 8 serving plates. Insert 3 potato crisps propeller fashion into the salad. Place chervil leaves on the plate between the potato crisps and stand 2 or 3 chives in the top of each salad for garnish.

*Sour cream may be omitted and
the amount of mayonnaise increased
to 2 cups if desired.

*The creamy texture of the dressing and the boiling potatoes matches the creamy texture of Chardonnay, while the sweetness of the shrimp and corn align with the fruitiness of the wine. If your wine is really big, rich, and intense, modify the recipe by substituting lobster for the shrimp, omitting the sour cream from the dressing and using the more powerful tarragon instead of chervil.*

Serves Eight

*This salad is so rich and immensely satisfying that your taste buds won't believe that it has less than one gram of fat per serving. It demonstrates how well beans can replace high fat ingredients in matching the buttery, creamy texture of Chardonnay. Add a pound of cooked shrimp to make it into a great summer dinner, still in the low-fat category.*

Serves Six
———

# WHITE BEAN AND SWEET RED PEPPER SALAD WITH FENNEL

1½ cups uncooked dried small white beans
1 large yellow onion, peeled, cut into quarters
6 cloves garlic, peeled
1 bay leaf
5 cups vegetable stock or 1 can vegetable broth with 3 cups water
salt and white pepper to taste
1 tablespoon freshly squeezed lemon juice
2 tablespoons balsamic vinegar
2 teaspoons Dijon mustard
1 tablespoon chopped chives
1 tablespoon chopped basil
1 tablespoon chopped Italian parsley
1 bulb fennel, core removed, thinly sliced
½ small red onion, thinly sliced
1 red bell pepper, thinly sliced
basil for garnish

1.  Rinse and sort the beans. Tie the onion, garlic and bay leaf in a cheesecloth bag. Combine the beans, cheesecloth bag and vegetable stock in a 3-quart saucepan. Bring to a boil and reduce the heat. Simmer for 1 to 1½ hours or until the beans are tender, adding water if needed to cover the beans.

2.  Drain, reserving the cooking liquid. Place the beans in a large bowl, discarding the cheesecloth bag. Season with salt and white pepper. Return the reserved cooking liquid to the saucepan. Cook until reduced to ¾ cup.

3.  For the dressing, whisk the reduced liquid with the lemon juice, vinegar, Dijon mustard, chives, 1 tablespoon basil and parsley in a bowl. Adjust the seasoning.

4.  Add to the beans with the fennel, onion and bell pepper and toss lightly to coat well. Garnish with additional basil.

# CORN AND RED BEAN SALAD WITH GRILLED SHRIMP

4 fresh ears corn*
1 cup cooked small red beans
4 green onions, white and green parts, sliced
3 tablespoons vinaigrette for Chardonnay (page 20)
4 medium cornichons, finely chopped
1 tablespoon capers, rinsed, drained
2 teaspoons Dijon mustard
2 tablespoons chopped fresh chives, tarragon and Italian parsley
1/2 cup (scant) mayonnaise
1/2 cup (scant) sour cream
6 to 12 butter lettuce leaves, or other salad green
24 peeled grilled shrimp**
12 chive spears for garnish

1. Cut the corn from the ears and combine with the beans and green onions in a bowl. Add the vinaigrette and toss to coat well.

2. For the remoulade, combine the cornichons, capers, Dijon mustard, chives, tarragon, parsley, mayonnaise and sour cream in a bowl and mix well.

3. Spread a spoonful of the remoulade in the center of each of 6 plates. Place 1 or 2 lettuce leaves in the remoulade and mound the corn mixture on the lettuce. Spoon the remaining remoulade to the side of the plates and arrange the shrimp around it. Garnish with chives.

*Make this dish when fresh corn is in season, as frozen or canned corn make a very poor substitute.

**During crawfish season, substitute crawfish tails for the shrimp, reserving 6 whole crawfish to garnish the plates.

*Although there are some similarities in the ingredients of this recipe and the Rock Shrimp Salad with Fresh Corn and Potatoes, this is much lighter, with a larger portion of corn and the use of a vinaigrette. The creamy textures of the beans and remoulade sauce make the textural tie, and the sweet corn and tarragon match the fruitiness of the Chardonnay.*

Serves Six as a First Course

*In the classic version of bread and tomato salad, stale bread is soaked in water and then squeezed out before combining it with the tomatoes. I prefer the flavor resulting from using lightly toasted croutons softened only by the juices of the tomatoes and the oil and vinegar. In either case, this recipe demands sweet vine-ripened tomatoes. In testing this recipe, I found that a locally baked potato-onion bread was particularly nice with the Chardonnay, but any French or Italian loaf with some density will work just fine. The use of a fruity sherry wine vinegar and the milder white pepper also help align this dish with Chardonnay.*

Serves Six to Eight

# PANZANELLA

1 loaf day-old potato-onion bread, French bread or Italian bread
3 tablespoons olive oil
1 clove garlic, mashed
2 baskets cherry tomatoes of various colors and shapes,
about 1¼ pounds
4 medium tomatoes, cut into 8 wedges each
1 cucumber, peeled, seeded, sliced
1 small red onion, finely sliced
12 fresh basil leaves, thinly shredded
½ cup extra-virgin olive oil
2 tablespoons sherry wine vinegar
salt and freshly ground white pepper to taste
6 to 8 basil sprigs for garnish

1. For the croutons, trim the crusts from the bread and cut into ¾-inch cubes; measure 6 to 7 cups of cubes.

2. Combine 3 tablespoons olive oil with the garlic in a glass measure. Microwave on High for 45 seconds. Discard the garlic. Drizzle the oil over the bread cubes in a bowl and toss to coat well. Spread on a baking sheet.

3. Preheat the oven to 350 degrees. Bake the bread cubes for 15 minutes. Toss the cubes to rearrange for even browning, removing any that have browned sufficiently. Bake for 10 minutes longer. Cool to room temperature.

4. Combine the cherry tomatoes, tomato wedges, cucumber, onion, shredded basil, ½ cup olive oil and wine vinegar in a large bowl. Season with salt and white pepper. Add the croutons and toss to mix well.

5. Spoon onto the serving plates and drizzle with any juices left in the bowl. Garnish with basil sprigs.

# Bulgur Salad with Summer Vegetables

2¹/₂ cups uncooked coarse bulgur
¹/₃ cup olive oil
1 cup chopped onion
1 cup sliced carrot
¹/₂ cup sliced zucchini
¹/₂ cup chopped yellow squash
1 cup sliced Japanese eggplant
2 cups peeled, seeded, diced tomatoes
1 cup water
salt and freshly ground white pepper to taste
¹/₄ to ¹/₂ cup extra-virgin olive oil
¹/₄ cup chopped basil
basil sprigs for garnish

1. Soak the bulgar in warm tap water in a bowl for 20 minutes; drain and set aside.

2. Heat ¹/₃ cup olive oil in a heavy wide saucepan. Add the onion, carrot, zucchini, yellow squash and eggplant. Sauté for 10 minutes. Add the bulgur, tomatoes and water.

3. Simmer for 10 minutes, stirring occasionally and adding additional water if needed to keep the bulgur from sticking. Season with salt and white pepper and remove from the heat. Test the bulgur for tenderness and let stand, covered, for 10 minutes longer if necessary for tenderness.

4. Cool to room temperature. Stir in ¹/₄ to ¹/₂ cup olive oil and chopped basil. Spoon onto serving plates and garnish with basil sprigs.

This dish is inspired by a recipe of Christophoros Veneris, chef and restaurant proprietor from Crete. The most important change I made in the recipe to align it with Chardonnay was basil rather than dill. Dill is a very difficult flavor to marry with wine, as it is at the same time sweet, sour, green, and pungent; a very slightly sweet Chenin Blanc is my choice for this herb. Although fresh tomatoes are often too acidic for Chardonnay, they work here because they take the place of the vinegar that might ordinarily be used to dress the salad. The tomatoes are therefore essential to the success of this dish, but any other vegetables on the Chardonnay food affinities list (page 53) may be substituted for the vegetables listed here.

Serves Six to Eight

61

I am not an accomplished bread baker. Being fortunate enough to live in Sonoma County with its many wonderful bakeries, I don't need to be. Pizza, however, is one of my fail-safe dinners when the cupboard is bare, so I had to figure out how to make an acceptable dough. Here is the simplest, fastest, no-brainer pizza dough. It does require a food processor and, if you get into this, you'll also want to invest in a pizza peel and baking stone. I buy unglazed 12x12-inch paving tiles for about $3.00 at a tile store instead of the more expensive stones sold in kitchenware shops.

Yields Two Twelve-Inch Pizza Crusts

—

# BASIC PIZZA DOUGH

1 envelope dry yeast
1 cup warm (110- to 115-degree) water
3 cups flour
1 teaspoon salt

**1.** Sprinkle the yeast over the water in a food processor container. Pulse once or twice to mix.

**2.** Add 1 cup of the flour and process until smooth. Add most of the remaining flour and the salt and process until the mixture forms a ball. Test with the finger and add the remaining flour if the dough feels sticky.

**3.** Knead lightly on a floured surface. Place in an oiled bowl, turning to coat the surface. Let rise at room temperature until doubled in bulk.*

**4.** Punch the dough down and knead lightly. Divide into 2 portions. Use immediately or store in the freezer until needed.

*If there is a time crunch, let the dough rise in a warm spot for 30 minutes. Otherwise, leave it at room temperature, as a slower rise allows for more flavor development.

Note: If I have time, I make 2 batches at once so I will have more ammunition in the freezer for future quick meals.

# CLAM PIZZA WITH BACON AND MOZZARELLA CHEESE

2 or 3 slices bacon
½ recipe basic pizza dough (page 62)
olive oil
cornmeal
4 ounces fresh mozzarella cheese in brine, cut into small cubes
2 tablespoons freshly grated Asiago cheese or Parmesan cheese
Chardonnay (optional)
salt to taste
16 small fresh clams in shells
freshly ground white pepper to taste
2 tablespoons coarsely chopped Italian parsley

1. Cook the bacon in a skillet until done to taste; drain. Chop coarsely and set aside.

2. Place a pizza stone on the lowest rack of an electric oven or directly on the floor of a gas oven. Preheat the oven to 450 degrees.

3. Roll or stretch the pizza dough to a 12-inch circle on a work surface; brush lightly with olive oil. Place on a pizza peel or the back of a baking sheet lightly sprinkled with cornmeal. Sprinkle the mozzarella cheese, Asiago cheese and bacon over the top.

4. Shake the pan or peel sharply to loosen the pizza and slide it onto the hot pizza stone. Bake for 10 to 15 minutes or until golden brown.

5. Bring 1 inch water to a boil in a small saucepan. Add a splash of Chardonnay and salt to taste. Add the clams, discarding any open clams or clams that don't close when lightly tapped on the counter. Steam, covered, for 3 minutes, checking every 30 seconds and removing any clams that have opened in order to prevent overcooking. Discard any that have not opened after 3 minutes. Remove the clams from the shells; cover to keep warm and moist.

6. Remove the pizza from the oven. Top with the clams and sprinkle with white pepper and parsley. Serve immediately.

Bacon is another wine-friendly food when used as seasoning in a dish. The slight saltiness balances with the acid aspect of the wine, and the little bit of sugar used in the cure aligns with the fruit. Melted mozzarella and plump steamed clams make the Chardonnay choice, matching its creamy mouth-filling texture.

Yields One Twelve-Inch Pizza

Pizza bianca, or white pizza, is actually a whole category of pizzas, the unifying principle being an absence of tomato sauce. I have come to prefer these pizzas, probably because most pizzerias in the United States use too much sauce for my taste. This is the simplest bianca, which makes it an ideal accompaniment to a very complex Chardonnay. The mild creamy cheese is in balance with the round mouth-filling texture of the wine, and the simple flavors don't fight the wine for center stage. If fresh mozzarella packed in brine is not available, substitute a fontina instead.

Yields One Twelve-Inch Pizza

———

# PIZZA BIANCA

1/2 recipe basic pizza dough (page 62)
olive oil
cornmeal
1 small yellow onion, sliced into very thin rings
4 ounces fresh mozzarella in brine or fontina cheese,
cut into small cubes
1 ounce freshly grated Asiago or Parmesan cheese
salt and freshly ground white pepper to taste

1. Place a pizza stone on the lowest rack of an electric oven or directly on the floor of a gas oven. Preheat the oven to 450 degrees.

2. Roll or stretch the pizza dough into a 12-inch circle on a work surface. Brush lightly with olive oil. Place on a pizza peel or the back of a baking sheet lightly sprinkled with cornmeal.

3. Arrange the onion rings and cheese cubes over the top; sprinkle with the grated cheese and season with salt and pepper.

4. Shake the pan or peel sharply to loosen the pizza and slide it onto the heated pizza stone. Bake for 10 to 15 minutes or until light brown. Slice and serve immediately.

# SPINACH PASTA

leaves of 2 ounces fresh spinach
1 egg
1 teaspoon salt
1 1/2 cups flour

1. Process the spinach in a food processor until finely chopped. Add the egg and salt and process until smooth. Add the flour and process until the mixture forms a ball.

2. Knead lightly on a floured surface. Let rest, covered, for 15 minutes. Roll to the second thinnest setting in a pasta machine, dusting with a small amount of flour if needed to prevent sticking.

3. Cut into desired shapes. Use in recipes such as the one on page 65.

# Chicken and Spinach Pasta with Pancetta and Tarragon

1 whole chicken breast, skinned, boned
2 cups unsalted chicken stock or low-fat chicken stock
1 cup Chardonnay
2 cups heavy cream*
4 ounces pancetta, or Italian bacon, chopped
1 medium onion, chopped
3 cloves garlic, minced
3 tablespoons butter
leaves of 1 small bunch spinach
1 tablespoon fresh tarragon leaves or 1 teaspoon dried tarragon
salt and freshly ground white pepper to taste
1 pound uncooked fresh spinach pasta (page 64)
tarragon leaves for garnish

1. Rinse the chicken well. Poach in the simmering chicken stock in a saucepan for 10 minutes. Cool to room temperature in the stock. Remove the chicken and cut into narrow strips.

2. Add the wine to the stock. Cook until reduced to 1 cup. Add the cream and cook until slightly thickened. Keep warm.

3. Sauté the pancetta, onion and garlic in the butter in a sauté pan just until light brown; remove from the heat. Add the chicken, spinach, 1 tablespoon tarragon, salt and white pepper and mix well.

4. Cut the fresh pasta into squares. Cook al dente in boiling water in a saucepan; drain well. Drizzle a small amount of the sauce on each plate and place 1 pasta square in the sauce. Spoon the chicken filling onto the pasta square and top with another square. Drizzle with the remaining sauce and garnish with tarragon leaves.

*For a lower fat alternative, omit the cream and add the reduced stock and wine to the chicken mixture just before tossing with the pasta.

Note: Commercial fresh spinach pasta or dried regular egg pasta is acceptable in this dish, but do not substitute dried spinach pasta. It is inferior in both flavor and color.

Chicken and spinach are wonderful foods that can go with just about any wine, but combining them with tarragon, butter and cream orient this dish to Chardonnay. Butter and cream will most often pair well with Chardonnay, with its buttery and creamy texture. Tarragon is a sweet herb which is well matched to the Chardonnay fruit.

Serves Four to Six

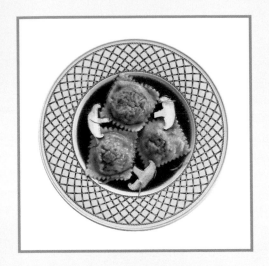

This is a wonderful dish for a big, deeply-flavored Chardonnay. It has equal intensity of flavor and body, but very little fat.

Serves Six to Eight

Pinot Noir becomes the preferred wine if you use darker, more deeply flavored mushrooms such as morels, chanterelles, or portobello in the ravioli.

# WILD MUSHROOM RAVIOLI WITH MUSHROOM BROTH

1 large onion, coarsely chopped
1 pound brown or white mushrooms, coarsely chopped
3 tablespoons unsalted butter
salt and freshly ground white pepper to taste
4 cups water     1/2 ounce dried porcini mushrooms
1 1/2 pounds assorted mushrooms such as shiitake,
crimini or chanterelles
1 small onion, finely chopped     3 tablespoons unsalted butter
1 clove garlic, minced     1/2 cup Chardonnay
1 tablespoon chopped fresh tarragon
2 tablespoons chopped Italian parsley
1 recipe pasta dough (page 64) or 1 package wonton wrappers
fresh tarragon leaves and 2 or 3 mushroom slices
per serving for garnish

1. For the broth, cook the coarsely chopped large onion and brown or white mushrooms in 3 tablespoons butter in a heavy-bottomed sauté pan for 1 hour or until caramelized, stirring occasionally. Season with salt and white pepper to taste. Increase the heat to high and add the water. Cook for 15 minutes; correct the seasoning. Strain and return the broth to the saucepan. Cook until reduced to 2 cups for a more intense broth.

2. For the ravioli, soak the dried porcini in hot water to cover in a bowl for 15 minutes or until soft. Drain and reserve the liquid; strain the liquid through a strainer lined with cheesecloth and set aside. Clean and chop the assorted fresh mushrooms and porcini medium-fine. Cook with the finely chopped small onion in the butter in a noncorrosive sauté pan over high heat until the liquid evaporates and the mushrooms begin to brown, stirring constantly. Add the garlic, wine and reserved mushroom liquid. Cook until the liquid has evaporated. Season with the chopped tarragon, parsley and salt and pepper to taste. Cool to room temperature; mixture should be quite dry.

3. Spoon the mixture onto half the pasta squares or wonton wrappers. Moisten the edges with water and top with the remaining squares, pressing to seal and eliminate air pockets. Place on baking sheets lined with lightly floured waxed paper. Chill or freeze until needed.

4. Cook in simmering salted water in a saucepan for 1 to 2 minutes or until tender; drain. Transfer to the hot broth in the saucepan with a slotted spoon and mix gently. Serve immediately, garnished with tarragon leaves and mushroom slices.

# SAFFRON RICE CAKES WITH FONTINA AND ASIAGO CHEESES

4 cups cooked Saffron Risotto (below)
2 ounces Italian fontina cheese    1 egg, lightly beaten
2 tablespoons unsalted butter
1 ounce freshly grated Asiago cheese
chives and basil sprigs for garnish

1.    For the rice cakes, spread the risotto on a buttered baking sheet and let stand until cool. Cut the fontina cheese into 8 to 12 small pieces. Combine the cooled rice with the egg in a bowl and mix well. Shape the rice into 8 to 12 cakes, enclosing 1 piece of cheese completely in each cake. Chill well.

2.    Heat the butter in a sauté pan until foaming. Add the rice cakes. Sauté over medium heat for 3 or 4 minutes or until a crust begins to form, shaking the pan every minute. Cook for 6 or 7 minutes or until a deep golden brown. Turn the cakes over and cook the other side. Drain on paper towels.

3.    Place 2 cakes on each warmed plate and sprinkle with Asiago cheese. Garnish with chives and fresh basil sprigs and serve immediately.

# SAFFRON RISOTTO

1/2 onion, chopped    1/4 cup unsalted butter
1 2/3 cups uncooked Arborio rice
1/2 cup Chardonnay
4 cups low-salt chicken broth
generous pinch of saffron
salt and freshly ground white pepper to taste

1.    Sauté the onion in the butter in a heavy saucepan until golden brown. Stir in the rice, coating the grains well. Add the wine. Cook until the wine evaporates.

2.    Bring the chicken broth to a simmer in a saucepan. Dissolve the saffron in a small amount of the hot broth in a small bowl. Add to the rice. Add the remaining broth gradually, cooking until the liquid is absorbed after each addition and stirring frequently; the rice should be just at the simmering point at all times. Season with salt and pepper to taste. Serve immediately or use for Saffron Rice Cakes.

*With butter and creamy fontina cheese in the ingredients list, you can almost assume that a buttery Chardonnay will be the appropriate wine choice. The creamy risotto also matches with the creamy texture of the wine. A big, full-flavored style of Chardonnay will best balance the intensity of the saffron. Because the rice cakes are so rich, I recommend serving them with a fresh tomato salsa or slices of vine-ripened tomato with some chopped fresh basil, salt and white pepper.*

Serves Four to Six

*Pumpkin and other winter squashes
can be wonderful with Chardonnay as
long as their sweetness is diffused
by the cooking method. The creamy
textures of the squash and the risotto are
well matched to the creamy buttery
aspect of Chardonnay. Fresh sage
has sweet herbal notes that complement
the fruitiness of the wine, but in dried
form it becomes much too strong.
If fresh sage is not available, use
Italian parsley instead.*

Serves Eight as a First Course

# ROASTED PUMPKIN RISOTTO WITH FRESH SAGE

8 miniature pumpkins*
salt and freshly ground white pepper to taste
8 fresh sage leaves
4 to 5 cups chicken stock
1 medium onion, chopped
3 tablespoons unsalted butter
1 1/2 cups uncooked Arborio rice
1/2 cup Chardonnay
8 fresh sage leaves, thinly shredded
1 cup freshly grated Asiago cheese
flowering kale and sage sprigs for garnish

1. Preheat the oven to 350 degrees. Cut a 1/2-inch slice off the tops of the pumpkins and reserve; scoop out and discard the seeds. Sprinkle the cavities with salt and pepper. Place 1 sage leaf inside each pumpkin and replace the tops. Place in a baking pan.

2. Bake for 30 to 35 minutes or just until tender. Cool to room temperature; discard the sage leaves. Scoop out the pulp from the pumpkins with a spoon, leaving the shells intact; reserve the shells and pulp.

3. Bring the chicken stock to a simmer in a saucepan. Sauté the onion in the butter in a heavy-bottomed saucepan over medium heat just until translucent. Stir in the rice. Add the wine and cook until absorbed. Stir in just enough hot chicken stock at a time to cover the rice, maintaining a simmer and cooking until the stock is absorbed after each addition and the rice is al dente. Stir in the shredded sage leaves and reserved pumpkin pulp. Correct the seasoning.

4. Reheat the pumpkin shells in the oven. Spoon the rice mixture into the shells. Place on serving plates and prop the top against the side of each pumpkin. Sprinkle with the cheese and garnish with flowering kale and sage sprigs. Serve immediately.

*If miniature pumpkins are not available, substitute a one-pound piece of a larger pumpkin and roast it covered with foil. Serve the risotto in warmed soup plates.

# SEAFOOD PAELLA RISOTTO

12 large uncooked shrimp
12 mussels
12 small clams
12 sea scallops
2 (4-ounce) andouille garlic sausages
3 tablespoon olive oil
1 small onion, chopped
1 clove garlic, minced
1 red bell pepper, cut into strips
1 large tomato, peeled, seeded, coarsely chopped
2 cups uncooked Arborio rice
1/8 teaspoon pulverized saffron
6 cups boiling water or fish stock
salt and freshly ground white pepper to taste
8 ounces fresh or frozen green peas

1. Peel and devein the shrimp, leaving the tails intact. Clean the mussels, clams and scallops. Set aside.

2. Cut 12 diagonal slices of the sausage 1/4 inch thick. Chop the remaining sausage into fine dice. Brown the slices in the heated olive oil in a wide heavy saucepan; remove to paper towel to drain. Add the diced sausage and onion to the saucepan. Sauté until the onion begins to turn brown. Add the garlic, bell pepper and tomato. Cook until thick, stirring constantly. Add the rice. Cook for 2 minutes, stirring constantly.

3. Dissolve the saffron in the boiling water or stock in a saucepan. Add the hot liquid to the rice mixture in increments to just cover the rice, adjusting the heat to a low simmer and stirring frequently. Cook until the rice is nearly tender and the liquid has nearly been absorbed.

4. Stir in the shrimp, scallops and additional liquid. Season with salt and pepper. Cook just until tender, adding the peas and 1 last addition of hot liquid. Arrange the mussels, clams and sausage slices over the top. Steam, covered, for 3 minutes or just until the shellfish open; discard any shellfish that do not open. Serve immediately.

*In Spain, people make paella with whatever they have on hand, so don't feel constrained to use the exact seafood specified here. Use anything listed on the Chardonnay food affinities chart (page 53) for seafood or poultry and expect a good result. The power of the saffron, combined with the creamy texture of risotto, calls for a big fuller-bodied style of Chardonnay.*

Serves Six

*This is a theme and variation on corn, which is a great partner for Chardonnay. The starch is rich on the palate, as is the wine, and the sweet flavors of the corn work well with the fruit character of the Chardonnay grape. Briny raw oysters are best with Sauvignon Blanc, but move into the Chardonnay field with the richness added from being dusted with cornmeal and quickly sautéed in butter.*

Serves Six

# Sautéed Oysters and Polenta with Salad and Roasted Corn Vinaigrette

1 1/4 cups yellow cornmeal
1 cup cold water
1 teaspoon salt
2 1/2 cups water
3 fresh ears corn
2 tablespoons unsalted butter
1/4 cup corn oil
1 tablespoon sherry vinegar
salt and freshly ground white pepper to taste
24 small oysters, shucked
1 cup yellow cornmeal
1/4 cup unsalted butter
6 ounces salad greens

1. For the polenta, mix 1 1/4 cups cornmeal with 1 cup cold water in a bowl. Combine 1 teaspoon salt with 2 1/2 cups water in a saucepan and bring to a boil. Stir in the cornmeal mixture. Cook over low heat for 5 minutes, stirring constantly. Spread 1/2 inch thick on a greased pan. Chill for 1 hour. Cut into decorative shapes with cookie cutters.

2. For the vinaigrette, preheat the oven to 450 degrees. Pull back some of the corn husks, leaving the base intact. Place 2 tablespoons butter on the corn and replace the husks. Roast for 20 minutes. Cool, remove the husks and cut the kernels from the cobs.

3. Combine 1/2 cup of the kernels with the corn oil and vinegar in a blender or food processor container and process until smooth. Strain into a bowl and season with salt and white pepper to taste.

4. Roll the oysters in the cup of cornmeal. Sauté the oysters and the polenta shapes in 1/4 cup butter in a sauté pan just until they begin to brown.

5. Toss the salad greens with the remaining corn kernels and vinaigrette in a bowl. Mound a handful of the salad in the center of each serving plate. Place 4 oysters alternating with 3 polenta cakes around the salad.

# Polenta with Wild Mushroom Ragout

1½ cups uncooked polenta     1 teaspoon salt
6 cups water     ½ ounce dried porcini mushrooms
1 small onion, finely chopped
3 shallots, minced     ¼ cup unsalted butter
4 ounces white mushrooms, sliced
8 ounces wild mushrooms such as shiitake,
oyster or chanterelle, sliced
½ cup Chardonnay     ⅓ cup chopped Italian parsley
1 cup heavy cream
salt and freshly ground white pepper to taste
Italian parsley sprigs for garnish

1. Whisk the polenta and salt into the water in a 2-quart glass bowl. Microwave on High for 20 minutes, stirring after 10 minutes.* Correct the seasoning and stir.

2. Soak the porcini in boiling water in a bowl for 10 minutes. Drain and chop the mushrooms, reserving the soaking liquid. Strain the liquid and reserve.

3. Sauté the onion and shallots in the butter in a sauté pan over medium heat for 3 minutes. Increase the heat and add the porcini and fresh mushrooms. Cook until the liquid evaporates. Stir in the wine and reserved mushroom liquid. Cook until the liquid is reduced to about ¼ cup. Add the parsley and cream. Cook until the sauce begins to thicken. Season with salt and white pepper.

4. Spoon the polenta onto warmed plates. Top with the mushrooms and garnish with parsley.

*To cook the polenta on top of the stove, simmer it for 40 minutes or until the mixture begins to pull away from the side of the pan, stirring frequently.

Note: For a more elegant presentation, make polenta cups by chilling the cooked polenta in a buttered 7x11-inch dish. Unmold and cut into six large rounds with a biscuit cutter. Make a well in the center of each round with a smaller cutter and scoop out with a spoon. Brush with butter and reheat in a 400-degree oven for 10 to 15 minutes. Fill the cups with the mushroom ragout and garnish with sautéed mushroom slices and parsley sprigs.

*Most people think of red wine with wild mushrooms. The lighter-colored varieties, particularly chanterelles and porcini, however, have a suave richness that is much better matched by a Chardonnay, albeit a big, powerful one. The sweet corn flavors of polenta pair with the fruitiness of the wine.*

Serves Six

# SEA SCALLOPS WITH TRUFFLED MASHED POTATOES

1 cup Chardonnay
2 cups veal demi-glace*
salt and white pepper to taste
1 1/2 pounds russet potatoes
1/2 cup heavy cream
1 tablespoon white truffle oil*
3/4 teaspoon salt
1 tablespoon unsalted butter
1 tablespoon olive oil
1 pound fresh sea scallops
sliced black truffle and chives for garnish

1. For the sauce, cook the wine in a noncorrosive saucepan until reduced to 1/2 cup. Add the demi-glace. Simmer until syrupy. Season with salt and white pepper to taste and set aside.

2. For the potatoes, peel and cut into halves and combine with salted water in a saucepan. Bring to a boil and cook for 20 minutes or until tender. Drain and press through a food mill.

3. Heat the cream in a saucepan until hot but not boiling. Add to the potatoes with the truffle oil and 3/4 teaspoon salt and mix until smooth. Keep warm in a covered double boiler.

4. For the scallops, heat the butter and olive oil in a sauté pan until very hot. Sprinkle the scallops with salt and white pepper to taste. Sear in the heated sauté pan for 30 seconds on each side or just until opaque and barely brown on the edges.

5. Reheat the sauce and pool a small amount on each serving plate. Stir the potatoes again and place a large spoonful of potatoes in the sauce. Arrange 6 scallops around the potatoes for a main course serving, and 3 or 4 for a first course. Garnish with truffle slices and chives. Serve immediately.

*Demi-glace and white truffle oil are usually available at specialty food shops.

# SEA BASS STEAMED IN CABBAGE LEAVES

1 cup Chardonnay
2 cups strong fish stock or bottled clam juice
2 cups heavy cream
2 tomatoes, peeled, seeded, chopped
5 to 7 savoy cabbage leaves
1½ pounds fresh sea bass fillets
salt and white pepper to taste
4 to 6 teaspoons fresh salmon caviar and
Italian parsley leaves for garnish

1.  For the sauce, cook the wine in a noncorrosive saucepan until reduced to ¼ cup. Add the fish stock. Cook until reduced to 1¼ cups. Stir in the cream and tomatoes. Cook over high heat for 5 minutes. Process with a hand-held food processor. Adjust the seasoning. Keep warm.

2.  For the sea bass packages, blanch the cabbage leaves in a large saucepan of salted boiling water. Remove to a bowl of ice water to stop the cooking. Pat the leaves dry and trim down the thick center vein to uniform thickness with the leafy portion. Place outer side down on a work surface.

3.  Cut the fish into 4 to 6 pieces and season with salt and white pepper. Place 1 piece of fish in the center of each cabbage leaf and fold into packages to enclose the fish.

4.  Line a steamer with the remaining cabbage leaf and place the fish packages on top. Steam for 15 minutes or until the fish springs back to the touch. Pat the packages dry gently.

5.  Ladle the warm sauce onto each warmed plate. Place a cabbage package in the center and garnish with the caviar and parsley.

*Cream sauce equals Chardonnay. Although this is not an absolute, it's a pretty good bet. Add sea bass, which has a buttery texture, and savoy cabbage, with its rich and mellow flavor, and you have a sure bet. Chardonnay will be a winner.*

Serves Four to Six

*Basil is one of the chameleon herbs. It can work with a variety of wines, depending on the other ingredients in the dish. With anything creamy, such as mayonnaise, it goes to Chardonnay. The richness of salmon matches the texture of the wine, and the sweet corn is balanced with the fruitiness.*

Serves Four

# POACHED SALMON WITH CORN RELISH AND BASIL MAYONNAISE

1 bunch fresh basil
¾ cup mayonnaise, low-fat mayonnaise or nonfat mayonnaise
kernels of 1 large fresh ear corn
½ red bell pepper, diced
1 green onion, dark green and white portions, sliced
1 teaspoon extra-virgin olive oil
¼ teaspoon sherry vinegar
salt and freshly ground white pepper to taste
2 tablespoons white wine vinegar
1 bay leaf      1 teaspoon salt
2 white peppercorns      4 salmon fillets or steaks

1.  For the mayonnaise, reserve 4 sprigs of the basil in plastic wrap in the refrigerator. Remove enough of the remaining leaves from the bunch of basil to measure ½ tightly packed cup. To set the color, dip the leaves into boiling water and remove immediately with a strainer. Plunge into cold water to stop the cooking process. Press gently to remove moisture. Purée in a blender or food processor. Scrape down the side and add the mayonnaise. Pulse just until well mixed. Spoon into a covered jar and chill in the refrigerator.

2.  For the relish, combine the corn kernels with the bell pepper, green onion, olive oil and sherry vinegar in a bowl. Season with salt and white pepper.

3.  For the salmon, combine the white wine vinegar, bay leaf, 1 teaspoon salt and peppercorns with enough water to cover the salmon in a wide saucepan. Bring to a boil and reduce the heat. Add the salmon. Simmer for 8 minutes for each inch of thickness, measured at the thickest point. Remove to a plate and cover with plastic wrap. Cool to room temperature.

4.  Place the salmon in the center of the serving plates. Spoon the corn relish on one side of the salmon; spoon a dollop of basil mayonnaise on the other side.* Garnish with the reserved basil sprigs.

*The recipe makes more basil mayonnaise than needed for the dish. Enjoy the leftovers on a tomato sandwich.

# SALMON STEAKS WITH SAFFRON-ONION SAUCE

1 pound onions, peeled, coarsely chopped
$1/2$ cup Chardonnay
$1/4$ cup white wine vinegar
$2^{1/4}$ cups unsalted chicken stock or reduced-salt chicken stock
$1/8$ teaspoon (about) ground saffron
2 tablespoons unsalted butter
salt and freshly ground white pepper to taste
4 to 6 salmon steaks
4 to 6 strips lean bacon
chervil leaves for garnish

1.  For the sauce, combine the onions, wine and vinegar in a saucepan. Cook over high heat until most of the liquid has evaporated. Add 2 cups of the chicken stock and the saffron. Simmer, covered, until the onions are very tender.

2.  Process in a food processor and return to the saucepan. Add the butter and the remaining $1/4$ cup chicken stock if needed for the desired consistency. Season with salt and white pepper. Heat to serving temperature and keep warm.

3.  For the salmon, cut the steaks away from the bones in 2 pieces, discarding the skin. Fit the 2 pieces together ying/yang style to form a circle. Wrap the circumference with the bacon and secure with skewers.

4.  Grill or pan-sear the steaks for 3 to 4 minutes on each side or until cooked through. Place on a flat surface and remove the skewers carefully.

5.  Spoon the sauce onto serving plates. Place the steaks in the sauce and garnish with chervil leaves.

Note: For a fat-restricted diet, omit the butter for a very satisfying sauce to use with shrimp or other lower-fat fish.

Salmon and bacon are high in fat and very rich in flavor, demanding a big, full-bodied Chardonnay with equal richness. The sauce, although low in fat, gives the impression of a rich beurre blanc, and the saffron flavor is equal in intensity to that of the other elements.

Serves Four to Six

*This is a brilliant recipe by Chef Craig Strattman. Though the sweet corn flavor of masa is well suited to a fruity Chardonnay, the typical tamale filling is not. The rich chicken and creamy Jack cheese are a perfect match with the rich and creamy textures in the wine. He strengthens the match by using butter rather than lard in the masa, evoking the Chardonnay's buttery flavors. The pine nut cream sauce makes a more formal presentation, but I prefer the tamales without the sauce.*

Serves Six
—

# CHICKEN AND CORN TAMALES

12 dry corn husks    1 whole chicken breast with bone
1/4 teaspoon sweet paprika
salt and freshly ground white pepper to taste
4 ounces Monterey Jack cheese, shredded
kernels of 2 fresh ears corn, about 1 1/4 cups
1 cup milk    3/4 cup unsalted butter, softened
1 1/2 cups masa harina
1 tablespoon baking powder
1/2 teaspoon salt    1/2 cup Chardonnay
1 medium shallot, chopped    1/4 cup toasted pine nuts
1 1/2 cups heavy cream    6 dry corn husks for garnish

1. For the tamales, preheat the oven to 450 degrees. Soak 12 corn husks in water to soften. Rinse the chicken and pat dry. Season with paprika, salt and white pepper. Place in a roasting pan. Roast for 20 minutes. Cool and chop the chicken, discarding the bones. Combine with the cheese.

2. Simmer the corn in the milk in a saucepan for 3 minutes. Strain, reserving the milk and corn. Measure 3/4 cup of the corn and set aside. Combine the remaining corn with the reserved milk and purée in a blender or food processor.

3. Whip the butter in a bowl until light and fluffy. Mix the masa harina, baking powder and 1/2 teaspoon salt together. Add to the butter with the puréed corn and beat until smooth. Fold in the reserved corn kernels.

4. Drain the soaked corn husks. Divide the dough into 12 portions. Place 1 portion in the center of each husk and press flat with the palm of the hand. Spoon the chicken mixture onto the dough and roll the husk to enclose the filling with the dough, tying the ends. Steam for 30 minutes.

5. For the sauce, combine the wine and shallot in a noncorrosive saucepan. Cook until reduced by 1/2. Add the pine nuts and cream. Cook until reduced by 1/2. Purée in a blender or food processor until smooth. Season with salt and white pepper to taste.

6. Cut the dry corn husks into decorative shapes and place on serving plates. Arrange 2 tamales on each husk. Spoon the sauce around the tamales and serve immediately.

# CHICKEN WITH BACON AND GREEN OLIVES

2 to 4 flour tortillas and vegetable oil for deep-frying the garnish
1 basket pearl onions, about 10 ounces
8 ounces bacon
2 whole chicken breasts, skinned, boned
3 cups low-salt chicken stock
1 poblano or other mild chili, seeded, julienned
20 to 24 pitted green olives
1 tablespoon arrowroot
Italian parsley leaves

1. For the garnish, cut the tortillas into halves or quarters and cut the rounded edges into a decorative pattern. Deep-fry in oil until golden brown. Drain on paper towels and set aside.

2. Blanch the onions in boiling water in a saucepan for 2 minutes; drain and cool. Peel and trim the ends, leaving enough of the root ends to hold the onions intact; set aside.

3. Cut the bacon into ¼-inch pieces. Sauté in a skillet until golden brown. Drain on paper towels and set aside.

4. Rinse the chicken well. Poach in the chicken stock in a wide saucepan for 10 to 12 minutes or just until cooked through. Remove the chicken from the stock and cover with a tent of foil to keep warm.

5. Add the onions, bacon, chili and olives to the stock. Cook over medium heat just until the onions are tender. Blend the arrowroot with a small amount of water. Stir into the sauce. Cook until slightly thickened, stirring constantly.

6. Cut the chicken into ¼-inch slices and add to the sauce. Cook until heated through. Stir in the parsley. Spoon onto serving plates. Garnish with the tortillas and serve immediately.

*Chicken is a natural choice for Chardonnay, but chilies are not. The idea here is to keep the chili addition minimal, so that it contributes the flavor of the chili but not the heat. If you love the hot stuff, go ahead and add more chilies, but save the Chardonnay for another occasion. If you can taste the wine at all, you will mostly taste just alcohol.*

Serves Four

*Both red and white wine go with quail, but a big Chardonnay is the choice here, with the wine and apple juice in the marinade and the fennel and hazelnuts in the stuffing. The apple juice and fennel reflect the fruitiness of the Chardonnay grape. The hazelnuts make it particularly nice with an older wine that has begun to develop some nutty flavors from the slight oxidation that has occurred.*

Serves Six

# GRILLED MARINATED QUAIL WITH ONION AND FENNEL STUFFING

MARINADE
1 cup Chardonnay    ½ cup apple juice
2 cups water    ¼ cup soy sauce
¼ cup packed brown sugar    2 tablespoons ground ginger
1 tablespoon dried basil    ¼ cup kosher salt

STUFFED QUAIL
6 quail    30 pearl onions, about 10 ounces
1 tablespoon unsalted butter    ⅓ cup Chardonnay
1 or 2 fennel bulbs, trimmed, about 10 ounces
celery leaves, parsley and thyme sprigs
1 cup low-salt chicken stock
½ cup skinned hazelnuts, coarsely chopped
salt and freshly ground white pepper to taste

1. For the marinade, combine 1 cup wine, apple juice, water, soy sauce, brown sugar, ginger, basil and salt in a noncorrosive dish and mix well.*

2. Rinse the quail and pat dry. Add to the marinade. Marinate for 1 hour. Drain the quail and air dry at room temperature for 45 minutes or in the refrigerator for 8 hours.

3. For the stuffing, blanch the onions in boiling water in a saucepan for 2 minutes. Drain, cool, peel and trim the onions. Cook, tightly covered, in the melted butter in a saucepan over low heat for 15 minutes. Increase the heat and add the wine. Cook, uncovered, until most of the liquid evaporates.

4. Discard the tough core from the fennel bulb and julienne the bulb. Tie the celery leaves, parsley and thyme into a bouquet garni. Add the chicken stock, bouquet garni and fennel to the onions. Bring to a boil and reduce the heat. Simmer until the liquid is syrupy, stirring occasionally. Add the hazelnuts. Cook until the liquid evaporates. Season with salt and white pepper.

5. Preheat the broiler or grill until very hot. Spoon the stuffing into the quail. Broil or grill for 3 minutes on each side for medium-rare or until cooked through.

*This marinade may be stored in the refrigerator or freezer and reused. Boil for 5 minutes and cool before using again. As a serving suggestion, make a nest for the quail out of risotto with any leftover stuffing folded into it.

# GRILLED PORK TENDERLOINS WITH CORN AND WILD RICE

1 cup uncooked wild rice
3 cups water     8 ounces bacon, diced
2 medium onions, chopped
4 ribs celery, chopped
1 cup Chardonnay
4 cups chicken stock or canned low-salt chicken broth
2 teaspoons chopped fresh basil
2 cups heavy cream     2 red bell peppers, chopped
2 cups fresh or frozen corn kernels
salt and freshly ground white pepper to taste
4 whole pork tenderloins
2 to 3 tablespoons olive oil
basil sprigs for garnish

1. Partially cook the wild rice in the water in a saucepan for 30 minutes. Drain and set aside.

2. For the sauce, sauté the bacon in a large saucepan until it begins to brown. Add the onions and celery. Cook over medium heat for 3 to 4 minutes, stirring occasionally. Drain the excess bacon drippings. Add the wine, chicken stock, wild rice and chopped basil. Simmer, covered, for 30 minutes or until the rice begins to split.

3. Add the cream, bell peppers and corn. Cook, uncovered, for 15 minutes or until the sauce begins to thicken. Add the salt and white pepper.

4. For the pork, preheat a gas grill or prepare a charcoal fire. Trim the fat and silver skin from the pork. Brush with olive oil and season with salt and pepper to taste.

5. Grill the pork for 2 to 3 minutes on each of 4 sides. Check for doneness with the point of a sharp knife; meat should still be slightly pink in the center. Grill for another minute or two if necessary, but do not overcook, as the pork will easily become tough and dry. Let rest for 5 minutes.

6. Cut a 2-inch portion for each serving and place in the centers of warmed serving plates. Spoon the corn and wild rice sauce around the pork. Cut the remaining pork into 1/4-inch slices and arrange on the sauce. Garnish with basil sprigs and serve immediately.

*This sauce, with its cream, chicken stock, and corn, aligns with the creaminess and sweet fruit in Chardonnay. The white meat of pork tenderloin is often mistakenly served with heavy red wines, but it is a much better match with a rich, intense Chardonnay. An equally delicious alternative is to serve this sauce with salmon and a lighter-style Chardonnay.*

Serves Eight

R O S É &

Pink wine has not always enjoyed a good reputation, and it IS fair to say that a lot of crimes have been committed in the name of Rosé, primarily by producers who consider blush wines to be for the "beginning wine drinker" who won't notice if the wine is less than perfect. However, it is worth searching out good blush wines, because they go so well with a wide variety of difficult to match foods, including those spicy chili-based dishes we all love so much.

What exactly is a Rosé or a blush wine? The classical version is a white wine made from red grapes. The amount of color and varietal flavor in the wine is controlled by the length of time the white juice is allowed to stay in contact with the red skins before pressing. Since we have no legal definition which demands this method in order to use the name, some producers simply mix together miscellaneous red and white wines, with unpredictable results.

When buying a blush wine, chances of finding a good one will improve if you choose one that names a variety of wine, such as Cabernet Rosé, White Zinfandel, and so forth.

In the profile of flavors and textures we taste in these wines, fruity is clearly the key word. Only simple, direct, fruity wines have the power to stand up to sweet and hot spices. The "sour" or acid component refreshes the palate, which is why the overly sweet styles of blush wines are not so successful with food.

B L U S H

## CHAMELEON RECIPES

# ROSÉ & BLUSH RECIPES

# Rosé & Blush Profile

## Food Affinities

| Seafood | Meat & Poultry | Herbs & Spices | Sauces | Cheese & Nuts | Vegetables & Fruits |
|---|---|---|---|---|---|
| anchovies | ham | allspice | barbecue | Asiago cheese | bell peppers |
| shrimp | prosciutto | black pepper | fruit | Parmesan | carrots |
| tuna | quail | caraway | vinaigrettes | cheese | corn |
| | sausages | cayenne | soy | almonds | cranberries |
| | smoked chicken | cinnamon | teriyaki | peanuts | fennel |
| | smoked duck | clove | | | figs |
| | smoked turkey | coriander | | | jicama |
| | turkey | ginger | | | melons |
| | | mild chili | | | oranges |
| | | nutmeg | | | pears |
| | | | | | raspberries |
| | | | | | strawberries |

## Food Conflicts

| Seafood | Meat & Poultry | Herbs & Spices | Sauces | Cheese & Nuts | Vegetables & Fruits |
|---|---|---|---|---|---|
| raw oysters | squab | dill | butter | blue cheese | artichokes |
| sole | veal | sage | citrus | Brie cheese | asparagus |
| whitefish | | | cream | Camembert cheese | green beans |

### Wine Flavors:
Zesty fruit: strawberry, cherry, raspberry, cranberry

### Wine Textures:
Sweet/fruity, sour/acidic

### Complementary Cuisines:
Mexican, Middle Eastern, Chinese, Thai, Cajun, Southwestern, and Indonesian cuisines are all good partners for blush wines.

### Best Methods of Preparation:
Grilling, roasting, braising, smoking

### Best Seasons:
Spring and summer are the seasons in which the freshness of blush wines are particularly enjoyable.

### Ideal Occasions:
Barbecues, picnics, Sunday brunches, and holiday turkey dinners with cranberries are perfect venues for blush wines.

There are probably as many recipes for borscht as there are countries in middle Europe. The one thing they all have in common, besides beets, is the sweet/sour component which comes from the addition of sugar and vinegar. Sweet/sour dishes will flatten almost any wine. Only a fresh blush wine has the sweetness and the liveliness, or acidity, necessary to match that of the borscht. This California version uses local dried tomatoes and balsamic vinegar. They provide not only the sweet and sour, but also an additional richness from their concentrated flavors.

Serves Six to Eight

___

# CALIFORNIA BORSCHT

1 pound boneless stewing beef
2 tablespoons vegetable oil
1 medium onion, chopped
3 quarts beef stock*
1 pound (about 3 large) beets, peeled, cubed
4 carrots, peeled, cubed
1/2 cup julienned dried tomatoes
1/2 cup balsamic vinegar
1 pound boiling potatoes, peeled, cubed
1 pound red cabbage, shredded
salt and freshly ground black pepper to taste
8 ounces sour cream

1. Cut the beef into bite-size pieces. Heat the vegetable oil in a heavy saucepan. Add the beef in batches with the onion and cook for 2 minutes or until light brown, stirring constantly.

2. Add the beef stock and bring to a boil; skim the surface. Add the beets, carrots, dried tomatoes and balsamic vinegar. Simmer, partially covered, for 30 minutes.

3. Add the potatoes and shredded cabbage. Simmer for 20 to 30 minutes or until the vegetables are tender. Season with salt and pepper. Ladle into soup bowls. Top with a generous spoonful of sour cream.

* Substitute half canned beef broth and half water for the beef stock if desired.

# Raspberry Rose Salad

3 edible pink or rose-colored roses
6 large handfuls of red leaf lettuces such as oak leaf,
lolla rosa and radicchio
5 tablespoons vegetable oil
1 cup fresh raspberries
1½ tablespoons raspberry vinegar*
salt and freshly ground black pepper to taste

**1.** Remove the petals from the roses and set aside. Wash and dry the lettuces and tear into bite-size pieces.

**2.** Combine the greens with the oil in a salad bowl and toss until well coated. Sprinkle with the raspberries, vinegar, salt and pepper and toss gently. Divide among 6 salad plates. Scatter the rose petals over the top.

*A raspberry vinegar made with a white wine base is preferable for this dish. Kozlowski Farms, in Forestville, California, makes an excellent one, and will ship it if it is not available in local markets.

*The colors, aromas, flavors, and textures of this salad are perfectly complemented by blush wines. The flavors and aromas of raspberries in the wine match the fruit, the sweet/acid balance of the raspberry vinaigrette matches that of the wine, and the whole is a symphony in rose pink. Finding roses that have been raised without herbicides or pesticides may take some effort, and I have even resorted to knocking on the doors of strangers with rose gardens, but the result makes it worthwhile.*

Serves Six

*Smoked chicken is an expensive food item available only in a few specialty gourmet shops. With this simple method, you can make it yourself any time. The only equipment needed are two 8x12-inch heavy foil pans and a broiling rack to fit them, at a cost of about $5.85, and a bag of wood chips at $2.29, which will fuel at least twenty-four smoking sessions. The delicate sweet-salt-smoke flavors imparted to the chicken by this process are a perfect foil for a fresh, fruity Rosé or blush wine.*

Serves Four
———

# EASY SMOKED CHICKEN

2 small whole boneless skinless chicken breasts
¼ cup packed dark brown sugar
½ teaspoon ground allspice
1 or 2 bay leaves, crumbled
¼ cup kosher salt or table salt
1½ cups fine hickory, apple or alder chips
½ cup (about) water

1. Cut the chicken breasts into halves; rinse and pat dry. Place in a noncorrosive dish. Mix the brown sugar, allspice, bay leaves and salt together. Rub over the chicken. Marinate, covered, in the refrigerator for 8 hours or longer.

2. Preheat a burner to medium. Cover the bottom of 1 of the foil pans with the wood chips. Sprinkle with the water.* Place a broiling rack in the pan. Arrange the chicken on the rack and invert the second foil pan over the top; secure with binder clips or paper clips.

3. Place the foil pan on the burner. Cook for 15 minutes, moving the pan on the burner every 3 to 4 minutes to heat evenly.

4. Remove the pan from the burner and test the chicken for doneness. Cook for 5 minutes longer if the chicken does not appear cooked through. Let stand, loosely covered, until cool. Serve immediately or store airtight in the refrigerator for up to 2 weeks.

*Vary the smoke flavor by the amount of water used to dampen the wood chips. For more smoke flavor, use less water.

# SMOKED CHICKEN AND FENNEL SALAD

8 sun-dried tomatoes in olive oil
1 tablespoon white wine vinegar
2 teaspoons Dijon mustard
salt and freshly ground black pepper to taste
1 whole smoked chicken breast (page 86)
1 yellow bell pepper
2 fennel bulbs (also known as anise)
3 cups thinly sliced red cabbage

**1.** For the vinaigrette, drain the sun-dried tomatoes, reserving 1/4 cup olive oil. Combine the reserved olive oil with the wine vinegar, Dijon mustard, salt and pepper in a bowl and mix well.

**2.** Cut the chicken into slivers. Cut the tomatoes and bell pepper into thin strips. Remove the tough core of the fennel bulbs, reserving a few sprigs of the fronds for garnish; cut the bulbs into thin slices.

**3.** Combine the chicken, tomatoes, bell pepper, fennel and cabbage in a bowl. Add mustard vinaigrette to taste and toss to coat well. Divide among 4 plates and garnish with the reserved fennel sprigs

*All of the ingredients in this main-course salad are slightly sweet, so it goes really well with blush wines, which lend to the slightly sweeter side. The acidity of the wine is high enough to easily handle the mustard vinaigrette.*

Serves Four as an Entrée

*Ordinarily, lamb wouldn't be served with a Rosé or blush wine, but the sweetness of the allspice and the red bell pepper make this the ideal match.*

Serves Four to Six

———

# MIDDLE EASTERN "PITZA"

¼ cup pine nuts
1 cup finely chopped onion
2 tablespoons olive oil
1 pound ground lamb
2 medium tomatoes, peeled, seeded, chopped
½ cup chopped red bell pepper
¼ cup chopped Italian parsley
2 tablespoons lemon juice
¼ cup balsamic vinegar
2 teaspoons tomato paste
½ teaspoon cayenne pepper
½ teaspoon allspice
½ teaspoon salt, or to taste
4 to 6 (5- to 6-inch) pita bread rounds

1. Preheat the oven to 350 degrees. Toast the pine nuts in a small skillet just until light brown, stirring constantly; set aside.

2. Sauté the onion in the olive oil in a large saucepan until translucent. Add the ground lamb. Cook until brown, stirring with a fork until crumbly.

3. Add the pine nuts, tomatoes, bell pepper, parsley, lemon juice, vinegar, tomato paste, cayenne pepper, allspice and salt. Simmer for 30 minutes or until the liquid is absorbed, stirring occasionally.

4. Split the pita bread rounds into halves and spread with the lamb mixture. Place on a baking sheet. Bake at 350 degrees for 15 minutes or until the edges of the bread begin to brown. Cut into quarters to serve.

# JAMBALAYA RISOTTO

6 (6-inch) andouille sausages
2 tablespoons butter or vegetable oil
1 cup (1/4-inch) ham cubes
1 pound boneless pork, cut into 1/4-inch cubes
4 cups chopped onion     1 cup chopped red bell pepper
6 shallots, minced
1 tablespoon minced garlic
1 tablespoon chopped Italian parsley
1 tablespoon chopped fresh oregano or 1 teaspoon dried
2 cups uncooked Arborio rice
1/2 teaspoon chili powder
1/4 teaspoon ground cloves     2 bay leaves, crumbled
1/8 teaspoon cayenne pepper
1/2 teaspoon black pepper
4 cups beef stock
1/2 cup Rosé/blush wine
1 tablespoon butter or vegetable oil
24 to 30 shelled uncooked shrimp
parsley for garnish

1. Cut 3 slices of sausage about 1/4 inch thick for each serving and set aside. Chop the remaining sausage into 1/4-inch pieces.

2. Heat 2 tablespoons butter in a large heavy saucepan and add the chopped sausage, ham, pork, onion, bell pepper, shallots, garlic, parsley and oregano. Sauté over medium heat for 15 to 20 minutes or until golden brown. Add the rice, chili powder, cloves, bay leaves, cayenne pepper and black pepper. Sauté for 5 minutes longer.

3. Bring the beef stock to a boil in a saucepan. Stir the wine into the rice mixture. Add the hot beef stock about 1/2 cup at a time, maintaining an even simmer and adjusting the heat if necessary to do so; stir occasionally. Cook until all the liquid has been absorbed.

4. Melt 1 tablespoon butter in a sauté pan. Add the sliced sausage and sauté just until the slices begin to brown. Remove to a warm bowl with a slotted spoon. Sauté the shrimp in the same pan until pink and cooked through.

5. Spoon the risotto onto warmed plates. Top each portion with the shrimp and sausage and garnish with parsley. Serve immediately.

*A true jambalaya may be so spicy that you won't taste the wine at all. I have reduced the quantities of cayenne pepper and chili powder in this recipe to bring them into balance with the sweetness of the cloves and the pungency of the garlicky andouille sausage. The result is a dish that sings with fruity blush wines.*

Serves Eight to Ten

*Blush wines make good companions to spicy foods because their simple refreshing fruit flavors can stand up to the power of the spices. The sweet spices in the Jerk Marinade align with the bit of residual sugar in the wine to enhance the pairing.*

Serves Six

———

# JAMAICAN JERK SHRIMP

JERK MARINADE
1 dried red chili pepper, seeded
1 onion, cut into quarters
4 green onions, chopped
3 tablespoons soy sauce
1 tablespoon vegetable oil
1 tablespoon white wine vinegar
2 teaspoons sugar
1 tablespoon fresh thyme
1 teaspoon allspice
1/2 teaspoon cinnamon
1/2 teaspoon nutmeg
1 teaspoon salt
1 teaspoon freshly ground black pepper
SHRIMP
1/2 recipe Jerk Marinade
1/2 cup olive oil
2 pounds shelled uncooked large shrimp
chives for garnish

1. For the marinade, process the chili pepper in a blender or food processor. Add the onion and green onions and process until minced. Add the soy sauce, vegetable oil, wine vinegar, sugar, thyme, allspice, cinnamon, nutmeg, salt and pepper; process until smooth. Store in the refrigerator in an airtight jar for up to 2 months.

2. For the shrimp dish, combine the marinade with the olive oil and shrimp in a bowl and toss to coat well. Marinate in the refrigerator for 2 to 8 hours.

3. Prepare a charcoal fire or preheat the grill or broiler. Drain the shrimp and thread onto skewers. Grill or broil for 2 to 3 minutes on each side or just until the shrimp become pink and opaque. Serve hot or at room temperature. Garnish with chives.

# Tuna Teriyaki

¼ cup peanut oil
1 teaspoon sesame oil
⅓ cup soy sauce
2 tablespoons rice wine or sherry
1 tablespoon grated fresh ginger
1 clove garlic, minced
2 teaspoons minced orange zest
4 fresh tuna steaks, at least 1 inch thick
soy sauce
carrot curls and sliced green onions for garnish

1. For the marinade, combine the peanut oil, sesame oil, ⅓ cup soy sauce, rice wine, ginger, garlic and orange zest in a bowl and whisk to mix well.

2. Pour the marinade over the tuna steaks in a noncorrosive dish and cover. Marinate at room temperature for 1 hour or in the refrigerator for several hours.

3. Prepare a fire for grilling or preheat the grill or broiler. Drain the tuna, reserving the marinade. Grill the tuna for 2 minutes on each side or until the fish springs back to the touch*, brushing each side at least once with the reserved marinade.

4. Place on serving plates glazed with additional soy sauce. Garnish with carrot curls and green onions.

*Fresh tuna should never be cooked beyond medium-rare, as it becomes very dry and loses most of its flavor.

Asian dishes with sweet elements such as ginger and rice wine are best complemented by fruity wines with a little residual sugar. Although Gewürztraminers are sometimes recommended for Asian cuisines, the spice of Gewürz is not harmonious with Asian spice and can taste bitter in the finish  A blush wine with good acidity wins, hands down.

Serves Four

——

An authentic turkey mole can be hot enough to overwhelm any wine, but in this recipe, I have eliminated the ground nuts and the searingly hot chilies which conflict with wine. With a moderate amount of chili powder added, a blush wine is needed to stand up to the spice.

Serves Six

———

Reduce the chili powder further, to become a flavor element rather than a heat element, and the dish becomes a true example of how chocolate and Cabernet can work well together.

# TURKEY CHILI MOLE

2 pounds ground or cubed turkey
2 tablespoons vegetable oil
2 cloves garlic, minced
1 large onion, finely chopped
1 (35-ounce) can tomatoes, chopped
2 teaspoons cumin
2 teaspoons coriander
1 to 3 tablespoons chili powder, or to taste
1/2 teaspoon dried oregano
1 piece cinnamon
1 1/2 ounces unsweetened chocolate
2 tablespoons red wine vinegar
salt to taste
1/2 cup chopped parsley and/or cilantro for garnish

1. Cook the turkey in the oil in a heavy-bottomed saucepan, stirring until crumbly. Remove the turkey with a slotted spoon.

2. Add the garlic and onion to the saucepan and cook over low heat for 2 to 3 minutes. Add the tomatoes, cumin, coriander, chili powder, oregano and cinnamon stick. Simmer, uncovered, for 15 minutes.

3. Add the turkey. Cook for 45 minutes or until most of the liquid evaporates, stirring occasionally. Stir in the chocolate and vinegar. Cook until the chocolate is melted and combined well. Add salt to taste. Spoon into serving bowls, discarding the cinnamon stick. Garnish with parsley and/or cilantro.

# ROAST TURKEY WITH CORN BREAD AND DRIED CRANBERRY STUFFING

1 1/2 cups dried cranberries, about 6 ounces
2/3 cup Rosé or other blush wine
2 cups chopped onion
1 1/2 cups chopped celery
1/4 cup butter
8 cups crumbled dry corn bread
1 1/4 cups chicken stock or turkey stock
2 eggs, lightly beaten    zest of 1 orange, chopped
1/2 teaspoon ground allspice
1/4 teaspoon dried sage
salt and freshly ground black pepper to taste
1 (14- to 16-pound) turkey
butter for rubbing the turkey

1. Preheat the oven to 350 degrees. Combine the dried cranberries with the wine in a small bowl and let stand to soak.

2. For the stuffing, sauté the onion and celery in 1/4 cup butter in a skillet over medium heat for 5 minutes or until the onion is translucent. Combine the onion and celery with the corn bread, chicken stock, eggs, orange zest, allspice, sage, salt and pepper in a large bowl.* Add the cranberries and wine and mix well.

3. Rinse the turkey well and pat dry. Stuff the corn bread mixture loosely into the neck and body cavities of the turkey. Tuck the wings under and truss the legs. Rub the turkey with butter and season with salt and pepper. Place breast side down on a rack in a roasting pan. Roast for 20 minutes per pound of turkey, basting every 20 minutes. (It is not necessary to baste the turkey at exact 20-minute intervals, but the more it is basted, the more moist it will be.)

4. Turn the turkey breast side up when 60 to 80 minutes of roasting time remain; the simplest way to turn the turkey is with the hands, using 2 clean hot pads. Roast until the breast is well browned and the juices run clear when the thigh is pierced with a sharp knife. Let rest for 20 minutes before carving.

*If a packaged corn bread mix is used, omit the sage, salt and pepper, as the mix is pre-seasoned.

With all the sweet ingredients in a traditional Thanksgiving dinner, the best wine choice is a fruity Rosé or other blush wine with a little residual sugar. The dried cranberries, orange zest and allspice in the stuffing make the turkey an integral part of the slightly sweet theme and also give an excuse to leave the cranberry sauce off the menu: I never did care for the stuff.

Serves Twelve

*When I first fell in love with wine, I would drink only Chardonnay or Cabernet Sauvignon. When I then fell in love with moussaka, I had a big problem, because neither wine tasted very good with it. A White Zinfandel saved the day, and also made me realize that there was a reason why they made these other varieties of wine. The sweet spices in this dish, which stripped all perception of fruit from the Chardonnay and Cabernet, were perfectly balanced by the slightly sweet and fruity White Zinfandel. Delicious.*

Serves Twelve

——

# MOUSSAKA

3 globe eggplant
salt to taste
2 pounds ground lamb
2 onions, chopped
1 clove garlic, minced
olive oil
1 cup fresh or canned tomato sauce
$1/2$ cup red wine
$1/4$ teaspoon cinnamon
$1/4$ teaspoon nutmeg
$1/4$ teaspoon dried tarragon
1 tablespoon minced chives
2 tablespoons minced Italian parsley
freshly ground black pepper to taste
2 cups shredded Asiago cheese
4 cups béchamel sauce seasoned with $1/4$ teaspoon nutmeg

1. Peel the eggplant and cut into $1/2$-inch slices. Sprinkle with salt and place on paper towels to drain.

2. Sauté the ground lamb, onions and garlic in a small amount of olive oil in a saucepan, stirring until the lamb is brown and crumbly. Add the tomato sauce, wine, cinnamon, nutmeg, tarragon, chives and parsley and mix well. Simmer for 20 minutes. Season with salt and pepper.

3. Pat the eggplant dry. Brush a skillet with additional olive oil and add the eggplant. Brown quickly over high heat and drain on paper towels.

4. Preheat the oven to 350 degrees and oil a 9x13-inch baking dish. Layer half the eggplant in the prepared baking dish. Layer the lamb mixture, $1/3$ of the cheese, the remaining eggplant and half the remaining cheese in the dish.

5. Spread the béchamel sauce over the layers. Sprinkle with the remaining cheese. Bake for 1 hour or until brown. Cut into 3-inch squares to serve.

# PICCADILLO

2 tablespoons olive oil
2 pounds lean ground beef
1 medium onion, chopped
1 clove garlic, minced
2 cooking apples, peeled, chopped
1/2 cup raisins
2 cups drained canned Italian tomatoes, chopped
1/2 cup slivered green olives
1 to 2 tablespoons chili powder, or to taste
1/8 teaspoon ground cloves
1/8 teaspoon ground cinnamon
salt and freshly ground black pepper to taste

**1.** Heat the olive oil in a sauté pan over high heat. Add the ground beef and cook until light brown, stirring to break up lumps. Reduce the heat and add the onion and garlic. Sauté for 5 minutes.

**2.** Add the apples, raisins, tomatoes, green olives, chili powder, cloves, cinnamon, salt and pepper. Simmer for 20 minutes, stirring occasionally. Serve over rice or rolled in warm flour tortillas.

*This is a traditional Mexican dish which is also used as a filling for tamales and empanadas. Fruity, high acid blush wines with their simpler flavors perfectly complement the mildly hot and sweet spices in Piccadillo. Note that the apples and raisins are simmered with the other ingredients until their sweetness is dispersed throughout the sauce. If the fruit were added toward the end of the cooking time, their sugars would be so concentrated that the wine would taste sour by comparison.*

Serves Six to Eight

PINOT

Pinot Noir is the classic red wine of the
Burgundy region in France. Most of us have
heard paeans to Pinot from the moment we got
interested in wine. Could it really be THAT good?
When it is good, it is very, very good; but it is
one of the most difficult wines to make, both in
the vineyard and the cellar. That means we
have to look a little longer to find a good bottle.
Those who make the search will be rewarded.
Whether light and fruity in style or deep,
complex, and earthy, Pinot Noir always displays
a characteristic elegance and a suggestion of
cherry/berry fruit that is seductive. With generally
lower tannins than other reds, Pinots tend to be
clearer and more delicate on the palate while
still delivering an intense red wine experience.
The delicacy of Pinot Noir can be easily
overwhelmed by highly flavored foods.
It is surprising that many consider lamb and
Pinot Noir to be one of the great matches
of all time, for the subtleties of Pinot Noir are
quite lost with the strong flavors of lamb.
This is NOT the wine to serve at a
blue cheese tasting.

N       O       I       R

## CHAMELEON RECIPES

Wild Mushroom Ravioli with
Mushroom Broth  84
Salmon Grilled in Fig Leaves  142

## PINOT NOIR RECIPES

# PINOT NOIR PROFILE

## Food Affinities

| SEAFOOD | MEAT & POULTRY | HERBS & SPICES | SAUCES | CHEESE & NUTS | VEGETABLES & FRUITS |
|---|---|---|---|---|---|
| salmon<br>tuna | bacon<br>beef<br>duck<br>game hen<br>quail<br>squab | basil<br>bay<br>black pepper<br>clove<br>garlic<br>lavender<br>thyme | butter<br>mustard<br>red wine<br>soy | Brie cheese<br>feta cheese<br>goat Brie<br>Jack cheese<br>Taleggio cheese<br>Teleme cheese<br>walnuts | beets<br>black-eyed peas<br>celery root<br>jasmine rice<br>kalamata olives<br>kale<br>mushrooms<br>mustard greens<br>pomegranates<br>red cabbage<br>red peppers<br>whole wheat<br>   pasta |

## Food Conflicts

| SEAFOOD | MEAT & POULTRY | HERBS & SPICES | SAUCES | CHEESE & NUTS | VEGETABLES & FRUITS |
|---|---|---|---|---|---|
| oysters<br>smoked fish<br>sushi | | cilantro<br>cumin<br>curry | cream | aged Gouda<br>   cheese<br>blue cheese<br>Cheddar cheese | artichokes<br>asparagus<br>green beans |

**Wine Flavors:**
Elegant to full-bodied; black cherry, berry, clove, violets, earth, smoky

**Wine Textures:**
Fruit, acid, slightly tannic/bitter

**Complementary Cuisines:**
Contemporary French and Northern Californian cuisines provide the clearly defined but delicate flavors that best suit Pinot Noir.

**Best Methods of Preparation:**
Grilling, roasting, braising, sautéing

**Best Seasons:**
Lighter styles of Pinot Noir are wonderful in spring and summer when lightly chilled. Save the full-bodied Pinots for the richer dishes of fall and winter.

**Ideal Occasions:**
Pinot Noir has the style to work equally well with an elegant dinner or a backyard grill.

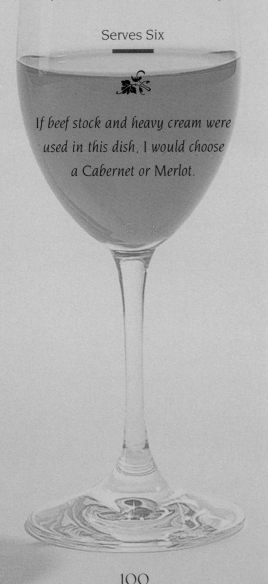

*I have always loved thick, hearty soups, and they are preferable with wine as they provide some contrast in texture. Using leftover bread as a thickening agent appeals to my thrifty nature as well as to my interest in low-fat cooking. It also suits Pinot Noir, which can be overwhelmed by dishes with a lot of fat. The chicken or vegetable broth also keeps the flavors in a more delicate range.*

Serves Six

*If beef stock and heavy cream were used in this dish, I would choose a Cabernet or Merlot.*

# MUSHROOM PANADE

3/4 ounce dried porcini mushrooms*
3 cups hot water
8 ounces shiitake mushrooms
12 ounces portobello, crimini and/or white mushrooms
1 large onion, chopped
2 tablespoons olive oil
1 clove garlic, minced
1 or 2 bay leaves
2 (14-ounce) cans vegetable broth or defatted chicken broth
1 teaspoon salt
1/4 teaspoon freshly ground black pepper
8 ounces stale French or Italian bread, crusts removed
1/2 to 1 cup half-and-half (optional)

1. Soak the porcini in the hot water in a bowl. Clean the fresh mushrooms with a brush or paper towel and reserve a few for garnish. Chop the fresh mushrooms.

2. Sauté the onion in the heated olive oil in a heavy saucepan over medium heat for 5 minutes, stirring occasionally. Add the fresh mushrooms and cook for 3 minutes longer, stirring constantly.

3. Add the garlic, the porcini with the soaking liquid*, the bay leaf and broth. Simmer for 20 minutes. Season with the salt and pepper. Stir the bread into the soup. Cook for 5 minutes or until the bread is moistened well. Discard the bay leaf.

4. Purée the soup in several batches in a food processor and return to the saucepan. Add the half-and-half and enough water to thin to the desired consistency. Heat just to serving temperature. Ladle into soup bowls. Slice the reserved mushrooms to top the servings.

*Dried porcini are available in Italian and specialty stores. If they are dirty, strain the soaking liquid through a sieve lined with a paper towel before adding it to the soup.

# BEETS WITH WINTER GREENS AND BRIE CROSTINI

1 tablespoon balsamic vinegar
¼ cup walnut oil*
salt and freshly ground black pepper to taste
¼ cup coarsely chopped walnuts plus 4 walnut halves
4 medium red beets or 8 baby beets
6 to 8 cups small winter greens
4 slices fine-grained whole wheat bread
2 to 4 ounces Brie cheese, at room temperature

1. For the dressing, whisk the vinegar and oil in a bowl. Season with salt and pepper.

2. For the salad, preheat the oven to 300 degrees. Spread the walnuts on a baking sheet. Toast for 15 minutes or until the walnuts begin to release their aromas. Cool to room temperature.

3. Cut the tops from the beets and reserve the smaller tender leaves to add to the greens. Cook the beets in boiling water in a saucepan for 25 minutes or until tender. Drain and cool. Peel and cut large beets into quarters or small beets into halves.

4. Drizzle a small amount of the dressing over the beets. Combine the remaining dressing with the winter greens, reserved beet greens and chopped walnuts in a bowl and toss to mix well. Mound in the centers of 4 serving plates.

5. For the crostini, trim the crusts from the bread and cut each slice into 4 triangles. Grill or toast the triangles. Spread with the cheese.

6. Arrange the beets and crostini alternately around the salad. Top with the walnut halves and serve immediately. Pass the pepper grinder at the table.

*Extra-virgin olive oil may be substituted for the walnut oil, but the flavor of the walnut oil adds particular interest to the dressing and is a better wine match. Since nut oils turn rancid very quickly, I recommend buying them in small quantities and storing them in the refrigerator.

*Salads for red wines require a little more thought, but they are entirely possible. Choose from ingredients that have deep, earthy, and/or bitter aspects for the best results. A little bit of fat, in the form of cheese, provides some density to anchor the combination, although the crostini can be omitted if you wish to reduce the fat content. For this salad, I have chosen deeply-colored winter greens, walnuts and beets. The sweet aspect of the beets works particularly well with the fruit flavors in Pinot Noir.*

Serves Four

*The combination of mushrooms and Pinot Noir is one of the more inspired food and wine matchings I've experienced. Although mushrooms are earthy, their flavors are not so strong that they overpower the subtleness of the wine. Searing them to serve over greens makes a bit of richness which anchors the salad and wine. The fat of a little shredded cheese is a nice balancing point for the acids and tannins in the wine, but it is not strictly necessary for the success of the pairing.*

Serves Four
——

# SEARED MUSHROOM SALAD

1 pound mushrooms, such as white, crimini, shiitake,
portobello, black chanterelle or morel
2 tablespoons olive oil
1/4 cup minced onion
1 clove garlic, minced
salt and freshly ground black pepper to taste
1 tablespoon balsamic vinegar
1/4 cup extra-virgin olive oil
1/2 teaspoon soy sauce
freshly ground black pepper to taste
6 cups mixed salad greens
1/3 cup shredded Monterey Jack cheese
1 tablespoon fresh thyme leaves or
chopped Italian parsley for garnish

1. For the salad, select one or more of the mushroom types. Clean with a brush or paper towel and cut into 1/4-inch slices. Heat the olive oil in a large sauté pan and add the mushrooms and onion in 3 or 4 batches.

2. Sear over high heat just until the mushrooms begin to brown, stirring constantly and seasoning with the garlic, salt and pepper. Remove from the heat and remove the mushrooms to a side dish. Repeat with the remaining mushrooms and seasonings. Return all the mushrooms to the sauté pan.

3. For the vinaigrette, combine the vinegar, olive oil, soy sauce and pepper in a bowl and mix well.

4. Toss the salad greens with 3 tablespoons of the vinaigrette. Divide among 4 serving plates. Top with the mushroom mixture and sprinkle with the cheese. Garnish with thyme leaves or parsley. Serve immediately.

# WINTER WHITE VEGETABLE SALAD WITH MUSTARD VINAIGRETTE

1 tablespoon Dijon mustard
2 tablespoons white wine vinegar
½ cup extra-virgin olive oil
Freshly ground white pepper to taste
8 ounces celery root
1 teaspoon lemon juice
1 teaspoon salt
8 ounces cauliflorets
salt to taste
8 ounces small boiling potatoes
4 small Jerusalem artichokes
1 large fennel bulb
cut chives or sliced green onion tops and
sprigs of fennel greens for garnish

1. For the vinaigrette, combine the mustard and vinegar in a large bowl and whisk until smooth. Add the oil 1 or 2 tablespoons at a time, whisking until smooth after each addition. Season with white pepper and set aside.

2. For the salad, peel the celery root and cut into fine julienne. Toss with the lemon juice and 1 teaspoon salt in a bowl. Let stand for 30 minutes.

3. Blanch the cauliflower in salted boiling water in a saucepan for 1 to 2 minutes. Remove with a slotted spoon and set aside. Add the potatoes to the saucepan and cook for 20 minutes or just until tender. Remove and cool; cut into cubes or thick slices.

4. Rinse the celery root in cold water and pat dry. Peel the Jerusalem artichokes and slice thinly. Remove the core from the fennel bulb and slice thinly. Add the celery root, Jerusalem artichokes and fennel to the vinaigrette and toss to mix well.

5. Add the cauliflower and potatoes to the salad and mix gently. Correct the seasoning. Serve immediately, garnished with chives or green onions and fennel greens.

Note: This salad looks great served on dark-colored plates.

*Winter vegetables are very satisfying with their density and crunchiness. They are also good for red wines because they are more neutral, with less acidity and less underripe green flavors. Avoid the sweeter ones such as carrots and parsnips, as they will make Pinot Noir taste dry and bitter. White wine vinegar is used in the dressing so the mustard flavor is clear, and also for aesthetic reasons: a balsamic/mustard mix would look muddy on these pale colors.*

Serves Four to Six

Lentils have a rich, earthy flavor that pairs well with the earthiness of red wines. Combining them with pasta lightens up their intensity, thus allowing the delicate complexities in Pinot Noir to shine through. This dish was inspired by a recipe in the first *Greens Cookbook* by Deborah Madison and Edward Espe Brown.

Serves Six to Eight

# WHOLE WHEAT PASTA WITH LENTILS

3 tablespoons olive oil
1 onion, finely chopped
3 cloves garlic, minced
3 medium carrots, peeled, finely chopped
1 rib celery, finely chopped
¾ cup dried lentils*
3 cups water
salt and freshly ground black pepper to taste
10 ounces stemmed chard or kale leaves
1 pound uncooked whole wheat rotelle or spiral pasta
3 ounces feta cheese, preferably goat feta

1. Heat the olive oil in a large heavy-bottomed saucepan over medium heat. Add the onion, garlic, carrots and celery in the order listed, cooking for 1 minute after each addition and stirring constantly.

2. Add the lentils and 3 cups water. Simmer, uncovered, for 20 minutes or until the lentils are tender and most of the liquid is absorbed. Season with salt and pepper to taste.

3. Cut the chard or kale leaves into 1-inch strips and stir into the lentils. Keep warm, covered, while the pasta cooks.

4. Bring a large saucepan of water to a boil. Add the pasta and cook using the package directions. Drain.

5. Add the pasta to the lentil mixture and mix well; adjust the seasonings. Spoon into warmed pasta bowls and top with the cheese.

*French lentils, especially from Puy, are worth looking for because they maintain their shape even when thoroughly cooked. Although the flavor of domestic lentils is equally good, they begin to disintegrate as soon as they are fully cooked and make a less attractive presentation on the plate.

# RICE AND LENTILS WITH WINTER GREENS

1 tablespoon balsamic vinegar
1/2 teaspoon soy sauce
1/4 cup olive oil
1/2 large onion, chopped
1 clove garlic, minced
1 tablespoon olive oil
1/2 cup dried lentils*
1 cup uncooked long grain rice
3 cups water
1 teaspoon oregano
1/2 teaspoon thyme
1/4 cup soy sauce
8 cups small winter greens
toppings of choice, such as seared tenderloin tips,
seared fresh tuna, sliced green onions, kalamata or
niçoise olives, braised or sliced uncooked fennel,
roasted red bell peppers, avocado slices

1. For the dressing, whisk together the balsamic vinegar, 1/2 teaspoon soy sauce and olive oil in a bowl. Set aside.

2. Sauté the onion and garlic in the heated olive oil in a heavy saucepan until translucent. Add the lentils, rice, water, oregano, thyme and 1/4 cup soy sauce. Bring to a boil and reduce the heat. Simmer for 20 minutes or until the liquid is absorbed.

3. Toss the greens with the dressing in a bowl. Select the desired topping ingredients and place each in a small serving bowl.

4. Divide the salad among 6 dinner plates. Spoon a portion of rice and lentils on top of the greens and serve immediately with the toppings of choice.

*Look for French green lentils from Puy in the gourmet section of your market. They are worth the price because they maintain their shape even when thoroughly cooked.

*This is an interesting one-dish meal that can be shared by omnivores and vegetarians together, as the meat or fish is served as a condiment at the table. Soy sauce has an affinity for many wines due to its saltiness and also, I believe, to flavor qualities that result from their both being products of fermentation. The earthy lentils and bitter winter greens reflect those flavors in the Pinot Noir, and the toppings are chosen with Pinot in mind.*

Serves Six

I get a real charge when a dish I invent out of whatever is on hand turns out to be a winner, as this pizza did. I had some leftover slow-cooked onions which I know are generally red-wine friendly. Duck sausage has the subtle rich taste that does not overwhelm a Pinot Noir, and the feta cheese has just the right amount of saltiness. A sprinkle of lavender-pepper aligns with the subtle floral notes in the wine. The big question was how it would taste all together. The answer was YUM!

Serves Two as an Entrée
or
Six as an Appetizer

# DUCK SAUSAGE PIZZA WITH ONIONS AND FETA CHEESE

2 onions, thinly sliced
2 tablespoons olive oil
salt and freshly ground black pepper to taste
1 duck sausage
1/2 recipe basic pizza dough (page 62)
cornmeal
1 tablespoon olive oil
1 to 2 ounces feta cheese, crumbled
lavender-pepper to taste (see recipe on page 143)

1. Cook the onions in 2 tablespoons olive oil in a saucepan over low heat until golden brown, stirring occasionally. Season with salt and pepper and set aside.

2. Grill or broil the sausage just until brown. Cool to room temperature and cut into thin slices.

3. Place a pizza stone or unglazed paving tile on the lowest rack of an electric oven or directly on the floor of a gas oven. Preheat the oven to 450 degrees.

4. Stretch or roll the pizza dough to a 12-inch circle on a work surface. Place on a pizza peel or the back of a baking pan sprinkled with cornmeal. Brush with 1 tablespoon olive oil. Top with the onions, sausage slices and cheese and sprinkle with a generous pinch of lavender-pepper.

5. Shake the pan or pizza peel sharply to loosen the pizza and slide it onto the heated stone. Bake for 10 minutes or until the crust is brown. Cut into 6 wedges and serve immediately.

# TELEME PIZZA WITH RED PEPPER AND CHARD

½ red onion, cut into wedges
1 red bell pepper, seeded, cut into ½-inch strips
1 to 2 tablespoons olive oil
salt and freshly ground black pepper to taste
½ recipe basic pizza dough (page 62)
1 to 2 tablespoons cornmeal
1 tablespoon olive oil
1 ounce stemmed chard leaves, cut into 1-inch strips
2 to 3 ounces Teleme cheese, cut into ¼-inch pieces

**1.** Place a pizza stone or unglazed paving tile on the lowest rack of an electric oven or directly on the floor of a gas oven. Preheat the oven to 450 degrees.

**2.** Sauté the onion and bell pepper in 1 to 2 tablespoons olive oil in a sauté pan over medium heat for 5 minutes or until nearly tender. Season with salt and pepper.

**3.** Stretch or roll the pizza dough to a 12-inch circle on a work surface. Place on a pizza peel or the back of a baking sheet sprinkled with cornmeal. Brush with 1 tablespoon olive oil. Distribute the chard and bell pepper mixture evenly over the dough; top with the cheese and additional black pepper.

**4.** Shake the pan or pizza peel sharply to loosen the pizza and slide it onto the heated pizza stone. Bake for 10 minutes or until the cheese melts and the crust is brown. Cut into 6 wedges and serve immediately.

*Because of its delicacy, Pinot Noir is a red wine quite suitable to vegetarian dishes. Some thought must be given to the choice of vegetables, primarily avoiding those which are high in acid. Cooking the red peppers reduces their acidity to make a really nice pairing with the fruit in the wine. Teleme is a delicate California cow's milk cheese which does not overwhelm the subtle complexities of the Pinot. If it is not available in your market, substitute Italian Taleggio or Monterey Jack.*

Serves Two as an Entrée
or
Six as an Appetizer

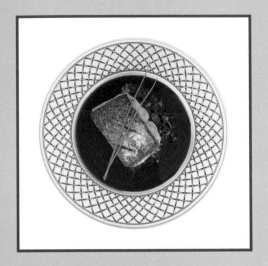

Salmon is a fish that can work with red wine because it is rich in flavor and has enough fat to carry it. Pinot Noir, being a more delicate red wine, is particularly appropriate. The mustard greens are slightly spicy rather than herbal, which complements the fruitiness of the wine.

Reducing wines for a sauce tends to concentrate their acidity, so a softening component is needed. Because Pinots can demonstrate a broad range of beautiful fruit flavors, I did not want to use a fruit syrup. I found that a little bit of balsamic vinegar and maple syrup took the edge off the acid while adding a very subtle complexity which does not overpower the wine flavors.

Serves Four to Six

———

# CRISPY SKIN SALMON WITH MUSTARD GREENS

2 cups Pinot Noir
1 tablespoon balsamic vinegar
1 tablespoon maple syrup
1/3 cup demi-glace
1 cup boiling water
salt and freshly ground black pepper to taste
1 (1 1/2-pound) salmon fillet with skin
1 large bunch mustard greens
2 to 4 tablespoons olive oil
1 clove garlic, minced
chives or sliced green onions for garnish

1. For the Pinot Noir sauce, combine the wine with the vinegar and maple syrup in a noncorrosive saucepan. Cook over medium heat until the mixture has been reduced by 1/2. Dissolve the demi-glace in the boiling water and add to the saucepan. Cook until the sauce begins to thicken. Season with salt and pepper to taste and keep warm.

2. Clean the salmon skin of any remaining scales and slash it lightly with diagonal strokes about 1 1/2 inches apart in a diamond design. Season skin side liberally with salt and pepper. Cut into 4 to 6 serving pieces. Remove the thick stems from the mustard greens and cut crosswise into thin strips.

3. Heat 1 to 2 tablespoons olive oil in a sauté pan large enough to hold the salmon. Add the salmon skin side down and cook for 3 minutes or until the skin is crisp. Turn the salmon over and turn off the heat; the heat in the pan will finish the cooking.

4. Heat 1 to 2 tablespoons olive oil in a large sauté pan or wok. Stir-fry the mustard greens and garlic for 1 to 2 minutes or just until the greens begin to wilt. Season with salt and pepper to taste.

5. To assemble, pour the sauce onto warmed plates. Divide the mustard greens among the plates and place a piece of salmon skin side up on the greens. Garnish with chives or green onions and serve immediately.

# Tuna with Onions and Sweet Peppers

2 fresh tuna steaks, 1 inch or more thick
salt and freshly ground black pepper to taste
1 tablespoon olive oil
2 large red or yellow onions, or 1 of each
2 red or yellow bell peppers, or 1 of each
2 tablespoons olive oil
1 cup kalamata olives, slivered
1 tablespoon coarsely chopped fresh marjoram or Italian parsley
4 soft rolls, split

**1.** Season the tuna with salt and pepper. Heat 1 tablespoon olive oil in a large sauté pan until almost smoking. Sear the tuna on both sides in the oil for 1 minute on each side or until brown. Remove to a platter.

**2.** Reduce the heat to medium-low and remove the pan from the stove to allow it to cool slightly. Cut the onions and bell peppers into 1/2-inch slices. Add to the sauté pan with 2 tablespoons olive oil. Cook until tender and light brown, stirring occasionally. Stir in the olives and season to taste with salt and pepper.

**3.** Cut the tuna into halves. Return to the sauté pan and cook just until heated through. Do not overcook the tuna; it should still be red in the center. Add the fresh marjoram. Place on the split rolls and top with the onions and peppers.

Variation: Cut the steaks into eighths and toss with 1 pound spaghetti cooked al dente. Top with bread crumbs toasted with olive oil. It can also be served at room temperature as part of an antipasto plate.

*Fresh tuna, cooked rare, or no more than medium-rare, is an excellent alternative to red meat for pairing with red wine. Its delicate, meaty flavor is particularly well suited to the subtle flavors in Pinot Noir. The sweet peppers and onions align with the sweet fruit elements in the wine and the subtle herbal notes of the marjoram give an interesting spark of contrast.*

Serves Four

*By cooking the tuna until it has just turned white throughout, the heavier, meaty flavor disappears, and you have a dish suitable for Sauvignon Blanc.*

The idea for this dish comes from Richard Allen, Chef of the Willowside Café in Santa Rosa, California. I tried this with a bottle of Pinot Noir and was blown away by the combination. Keep your eyes peeled for pomegranates in the market in November and December and jump on this. The pomegranate has just the right amount of delicate fruit and acidity to match that of the wine, giving a lift to the richness of the duck. The quick stir-frying of the Brussels sprout leaves results in a totally different impression of this member of the cabbage family. The leaves are fresh and green in color, but retain the more neutral flavor of cabbage, which does not conflict with red wine.

Serves Four

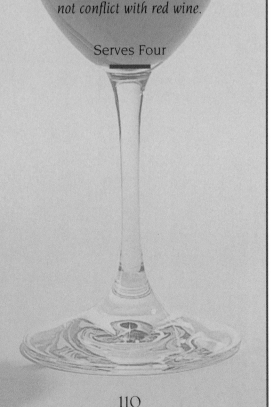

# ROASTED DUCK LEGS WITH POMEGRANATE

4 duck legs with thighs
salt and freshly ground black pepper to taste
1 pomegranate
8 ounces Brussels sprouts
4 slices lean bacon, cut into ¼-inch strips
¼ cup duck or chicken stock
1 tablespoon balsamic vinegar
2 tablespoons unsweetened pomegranate juice

1. Preheat the oven to 400 degrees. Rinse the duck and pat dry. Season with salt and pepper. Place skin side down in a heated sauté pan.* Cook over medium heat until golden brown on both sides.

2. Remove the duck to a small roasting pan. Roast for 40 to 60 minutes or until very tender and crisp.

3. Break open the pomegranate; separate and reserve the seeds. Remove the green outer leaves of the Brussels sprouts, reserving the cores for the soup pot.

4. Wipe the sauté pan used for browning the duck. Add the bacon to the pan and sauté until golden brown. Remove to a paper towel with a slotted spoon. Drain the pan, reserving 2 tablespoons drippings.

5. Stir-fry the Brussels sprouts leaves in the reserved drippings for 1 to 2 minutes. Add the stock, vinegar and pomegranate juice. Cook for 1 minute longer, stirring constantly; leaves should remain dark green. Add the bacon and pepper to taste.

6. Spoon onto warmed plates. Place the duck on top and sprinkle with the reserved pomegranate seeds. Serve immediately.

*Because duck has a lot of fat, additional cooking oil is not needed.

Note: Pomegranate juice is usually available at health food stores.

# ASIAN-FLAVOR BEEF ROLLS

1 cup shredded red cabbage, about 3 ounces
1 tablespoon rice wine vinegar
1 teaspoon mirin (rice wine) or sherry
1/2 teaspoon soy sauce
6 ounces beef tenderloin tips or other lean beef
2 to 3 tablespoons soy sauce
4 whole wheat flour tortillas
3 ounces shiitake mushroom caps, sliced
1 tablespoon vegetable oil
2 tablespoons water
1/4 teaspoon sugar
1 tablespoon soy sauce
freshly ground black pepper to taste
1 teaspoon vegetable oil
1/4 cucumber, peeled, cut into 1/4-inch sticks, about 3 ounces
2 green onions, trimmed to 4 inches, cut lengthwise into quarters
1/2 avocado, thinly sliced lengthwise
green onions for garnish

**1.** Combine the cabbage with the vinegar, mirin and 1/2 teaspoon soy sauce in a bowl. Combine the beef with 2 to 3 tablespoons soy sauce in a bowl, turning to coat well. Marinate the cabbage and beef at room temperature.

**2.** Preheat the oven to 300 degrees. Wrap the tortillas in foil. Place in the oven to heat.

**3.** Sauté the mushrooms in 1 tablespoon heated vegetable oil in a sauté pan just until they begin to brown. Add the water, sugar and 1 tablespoon soy sauce. Cook until the liquid has evaporated, stirring frequently.

**4.** Drain the beef, reserving the marinade; season the beef with pepper. Sear in a sauté pan heated with 1 teaspoon vegetable oil until brown on all sides. Pour the reserved marinade over the beef, stirring to deglaze the sauté pan. Cut the beef into thin strips; keep warm.

**5.** Spoon the mushrooms down the center of each tortilla. Add the cabbage, cucumber, green onions, avocado and beef. Roll the tortillas as tightly as possible to enclose the filling.

**6.** Cut each roll diagonally into halves. Prop one on top of the other on serving plates. Garnish with additional green onions.

*Pinot Noir is one of the few red wines that can work with Asian seasonings, because it tends to be fruity and lower in tannin. The clarity of the flavors of the beef and uncooked vegetables in this dish is subtle and does not overwhelm the delicate flavors in the wine. I chose the tortillas, rather than an Asian wrapper, for the Pinot because of the delicate earthiness of the whole wheat.*

Serves Four

111

*I find that the big, full-bodied Chardonnays often make the best pairing with pork tenderloin, which is a white meat. However, I thought it might work with Pinot Noir, which is easily overwhelmed by strong flavors. Using a red-wine marinade for the pork, and braising it with red cabbage, it easily makes the transition.*

Serves Six

# PORK TENDERLOINS BRAISED WITH RED CABBAGE

3 pork tenderloins     1 cup Pinot Noir
1/2 cup olive oil
1 tablespoon balsamic vinegar
2 bay leaves, crumbled
2 cloves garlic, mashed
ground cloves     2 tablespoons olive oil
3 thick slices bacon
1 large red onion, thinly sliced
4 medium carrots, peeled, sliced or julienned
1 (2-pound) red cabbage, cored, thinly shredded
1/2 cup beef stock or canned beef broth
1 teaspoon salt
1/8 teaspoon freshly ground black pepper
steamed baby carrots for garnish

1.  Trim the tenderloins of all fat and silver skin. Combine the Pinot Noir, 1/2 cup olive oil, balsamic vinegar, bay leaves, garlic and a pinch of ground cloves in a noncorrosive bowl and whisk to mix well. Add the tenderloin and turn to coat well. Marinate, covered, at room temperature for 1 hour or in the refrigerator for 8 hours or longer, turning 2 or 3 times.

2.  Remove the tenderloins to drain on paper towels, reserving the marinade. Cut the tenderloins into halves. Brown in 2 tablespoons olive oil in a large heavy sauté pan. Remove the pork.

3.  Cut the bacon into 1/4-inch strips. Add to the sauté pan. Cook over low heat just until light brown. Add the onion and sliced or julienned carrots. Cook for 3 or 4 minutes, stirring occasionally. Add the cabbage. Cook until it begins to wilt.

4.  Add the reserved marinade with the garlic, beef stock, salt and pepper and mix well. Add the pork, covering with the cabbage. Cook, covered, over low heat for 10 minutes, turning the pork 1 time.

5.  Remove the pork to a plate. Cook the cabbage, uncovered, until the liquid is reduced to a syrup if a lot of liquid still remains. Adjust the seasonings.

6.  Slice the pork. Spoon the cabbage onto warmed plates. Arrange the pork over the top. Garnish with steamed baby carrots.

# BEEF BROCHETTES WITH BLACK-EYED PEAS

1 1/2 cups dried black-eyed peas
4 cups cold water    7 slices lean bacon
1 clove garlic, minced    1 large onion, chopped
3 carrots, peeled, chopped    1/2 teaspoon salt
freshly ground black pepper to taste
6 (10-inch) bamboo skewers
4 Japanese eggplant    12 (1 1/4-inch) mushrooms
2 tablespoons olive oil    salt to taste
10 ounces trimmed beef tenderloin tips or other lean beef
1/4 cup coarsely chopped Italian parsley
parsley sprigs for garnish

1. Rinse and sort the dried peas. Combine with the cold water in a saucepan. Cook for 40 minutes or until nearly tender.

2. Sauté the bacon in a sauté pan until light brown but still flexible. Remove the bacon to a paper towel to drain. Chop 3 of the slices and reserve the remaining slices. Drain the sauté pan, reserving 3 tablespoons drippings in the pan.

3. Add the garlic, onion and carrots to the sauté pan. Sauté over medium-low heat until tender but not brown. Stir in the chopped bacon. Set aside.

4. Pour most of the excess water off of the peas. Add the onion and carrot mixture. Cook until the peas are tender and the remaining liquid has evaporated. Season with 1/2 teaspoon salt and pepper to taste. Keep warm.

5. Preheat the broiler or grill. Place the skewers in water to soak. Cut the eggplant crosswise into 18 even slices. Clean the mushrooms with a brush or paper towel and discard the stems. Toss the eggplant and mushroom caps with the olive oil in a bowl. Sprinkle with salt and pepper to taste.

6. Cut the reserved bacon into thirds. Cut the beef into 12 equal pieces and wrap with the bacon. Assemble the brochettes starting with a slice of eggplant, then a piece of beef and a mushroom cap. Repeat the process and finish with another slice of eggplant.

7. Grill for 10 minutes or until browned on all sides and the beef is cooked through. Stir the chopped parsley into the peas. Spoon into the center of warmed serving plates. Top with a brochette and garnish with a sprig of parsley.

*The earthier flavors of whole grains go very well with red wines in general. The subtleness of Pinot Noir, however, can be overwhelmed by strong flavors and textures. Black-eyed peas are perfect because their earthy aspect is subtle. They also have a slight sweetness which works very well with the fruit aspects of Pinot. The components of the brochettes have uncomplicated clear flavors of medium intensity, which show the wine to its best advantage.*

Serves Four to Six

*You can make a match with Cabernet or Merlot by serving the brochettes with the deeper, earthier flavors of the braised lentils on page 140.*

113

Z  I  N  F  A

This is a test. What color is Zinfandel?
If you answered red, you may now be inducted
into the serious wine geek club. If you answered
white or pink, please refer to the chapter on
Rosé and Blush Wines.

Zinfandel at its best is a lush, fruity red wine
with intense aromas and flavors of wild
blackberries or black raspberries. It can have a
tannic structure equal to that of Cabernet
Sauvignon, and these wines have sometimes
been used as "ringers" in blind tastings of
Cabernet. However, Zinfandel does not age as
well as Cabernet, because it lacks the additional
complexities of flavor that give Cabernet
interest after the fruit flavors begin to fade.
Zinfandels can also be slightly sweet, or very
high in alcohol, as the grape ripens so fast that
it is hard to pick a vineyard without the sugars
escalating to higher than desirable levels.
The berry fruit flavors of Zinfandel make it a wine
that can handle a little bit of heat in the spice
department, and it is particularly well suited
to dishes based on cooked tomatoes.

N          D          E          L

# ZINFANDEL RECIPES

# ZINFANDEL PROFILE

| Food Affinities | | | | | |
|---|---|---|---|---|---|
| **SEAFOOD** | **MEAT & POULTRY** | **HERBS & SPICES** | **SAUCES** | **CHEESE & NUTS** | **VEGETABLES & FRUITS** |
| crab<br>hot-smoked<br>  salmon<br>mussels<br>shrimp | bacon<br>beef<br>chicken<br>pork<br>quail<br>sausage | basil<br>bay leaf<br>filé<br>mild chili<br>oregano<br>paprika | balsamic<br>barbecue<br>mild salsa<br>tomato | aged goat<br>  cheese<br>blue cheese<br>dry Jack cheese<br>Parmesan<br>  cheese | blackberries<br>corn/polenta<br>dried tomatoes<br>eggplant<br>figs<br>tomatoes<br>zucchini |

| Food Conflicts | | | | | |
|---|---|---|---|---|---|
| **SEAFOOD** | **MEAT & POULTRY** | **HERBS & SPICES** | **SAUCES** | **CHEESE & NUTS** | **VEGETABLES & FRUITS** |
| raw oysters<br>sardines<br>sole<br>sushi<br>whitefish | pheasant<br>smoked chicken<br>veal | capers<br>cumin<br>curry<br>dill | butter<br>citrus<br>cream<br>mayonnaise<br>velouté | aged Gouda<br>  cheese<br>Swiss cheese<br>pecans | artichokes<br>asparagus<br>green beans |

**Wine Flavors:**
Wild blackberries, raspberries, raisins, prunes, licorice, black pepper, chocolate, violets

**Wine Textures:**
fruity/sweet, tannic/bitter, both fruity and tannic, acid

**Complementary Cuisines:**
Robust cuisines, particularly those that are tomato based, such as southern Italian, Creole, Southwestern, and barbecue from almost anywhere in the United States.

**Best Methods of Preparation:**
Stews, braising, grilling, barbecue

**Best Seasons:**
Drink Zinfandel in late summer and fall, when the sun is warm and tomatoes are at their best.

**Ideal Occasions:**
Zinfandel's simple but robust style is fitting for everyday drinking and barbecues.

Roasting tomatoes concentrates their flavors in a way that can't be duplicated by cooking them on top of the stove. Even out of season tomatoes respond to this method. The result is an intensely flavored soup that can have almost zero fat. A fruit-packed Zinfandel easily handles the tomato fruit, and the spiciness of the wine deflects the acidity of the tomatoes. The fat of a little shredded Italian fontina is nice with the wine, but can be omitted by those who are seriously watching their fat intake.

Serves Four

# ROASTED TOMATO SOUP

2½ pounds fresh tomatoes
olive oil
salt and freshly ground black pepper
1 large onion, chopped
2 cloves garlic, minced
2 tablespoons olive oil
2 cups nonfat chicken broth or vegetable broth
2 tablespoons shredded Italian fontina cheese

1. Preheat the oven to 350 degrees. Remove the stem core from the tomatoes and cut into ³/₈-inch slices. Brush 1 or 2 baking pans with olive oil and sprinkle with salt and pepper. Arrange the tomato slices in the prepared pans; brush the tops with olive oil and sprinkle with salt and pepper.

2. Roast the tomatoes for 30 minutes. Turn the slices over and roast for 30 minutes longer or until they are just beginning to color at the edges of the baking pan.

3. Sauté the onion and garlic in 2 tablespoons heated olive oil in a saucepan for 5 minutes or until tender but not brown. Stir in the roasted tomatoes. Add the broth. Cook, covered, over low heat, for 20 minutes.

4. Purée and put through a food mill or coarse strainer. Return to the saucepan and heat to serving temperature. Correct the seasoning and serve immediately sprinkled with the fontina cheese.

# Aged Goat Cheese with Figs and Belgian Endive

3 dried figs, cut into halves
1/2 cup Zinfandel
1 teaspoon balsamic vinegar
3 heads Belgian endive
2 tablespoons extra-virgin olive oil
salt and freshly cracked black pepper to taste
4 to 6 ounces aged goat cheese*

1. Combine the dried figs with the wine and just enough water to cover in a small nonreactive saucepan. Poach over medium-low heat for 10 minutes or just until the figs are tender, adding additional water if needed to cover the figs. Cool in the poaching liquid.

2. Drain the figs and cut into halves again. Scrape the seeds and pulp away from the flesh and discard. Cut the flesh into fine julienne. Toss with the balsamic vinegar in a small bowl and set aside.

3. Core the endive and cut into fine julienne. Combine the endive, figs and olive oil in a salad bowl and toss lightly. Season with salt and pepper. Divide among 6 plates. Cut the cheese into 18 pieces and arrange 3 pieces on each serving.

*Laura Chenel's Taupiniere is a good choice for the cheese in the recipe.

The inspiration for this recipe came from a dish I had at Babette's Restaurant in the town of Sonoma. I modified the sweetness of the dried figs by poaching them in a little of the wine so they would not overwhelm the panoply of fruit flavors that a good Zinfandel provides. The fruit is further balanced by the pungent aged goat cheese, and the slight bitterness of Belgian endive aligns with the tannins to cut through the richness of the fruit and cheese.

Serves Six

*Zinfandel and tomatoes make a winning combination in general. However, the sugar in tomatoes becomes very concentrated when they are dried. If added to a dish whole or in large pieces, this concentrated sweetness will overwhelm even a very fruity Zinfandel, leaving it dry, bitter and/or sour. Mincing the dried tomatoes disperses the sweetness, which is additionally balanced by the acid of the vinegar. The result is another great pairing of tomato and Zinfandel.*

Serves Six

# GREEN SALAD WITH SUN-DRIED TOMATO VINAIGRETTE

1 ounce sun-dried tomatoes
¼ cup extra-virgin olive oil
1 tablespoon balsamic vinegar
salt and freshly ground black pepper to taste
6 large handfuls of mixed small lettuces
2 tablespoons chopped fresh oregano, Italian parsley
and/or basil for garnish

1. Cover the dried tomatoes with boiling water in a heat-proof bowl. Let stand at room temperature until completely softened; drain on paper towels. Mince finely.

2. Combine the tomatoes with the olive oil in a bowl. Marinate for several minutes if time permits. Whisk in the vinegar, salt and pepper.

3. Toss with the greens in a bowl. Divide among 6 salad plates. Sprinkle with the fresh herbs.

# SPAGHETTI WITH MEAT SAUCE

1 pound sweet or hot Italian sausage
1/4 cup olive oil
1 pound ground beef
1 large onion, chopped
1 red bell pepper, seeded, chopped
1 clove garlic, chopped
1 (28-ounce) can peeled tomatoes, chopped
1/2 cup Zinfandel
1 bay leaf
1 tablespoon dried oregano
1 teaspoon salt
1/2 teaspoon freshly ground black pepper
1 (6-ounce) can tomato paste (optional)
salt to taste
1 1/2 pounds uncooked dried spaghetti
2 tablespoons fresh pesto or chopped fresh basil
freshly grated Parmesan cheese

1. Remove the sausage from its casing. Cook in the heated olive oil in a wide heavy saucepan for 3 minutes, stirring to break up the sausage. Add the ground beef and cook just until it begins to brown, stirring to crumble. Add the onion, bell pepper and garlic. Cook for 3 to 4 minutes longer, stirring constantly.

2. Add the undrained tomatoes, wine, bay leaf, oregano, 1 teaspoon salt and pepper. Stir in the tomato paste if desired. Cook over low heat for 1 hour, stirring occasionally.*

3. Bring a large saucepan of water to a boil and add salt to taste. Add the pasta. Cook for 10 to 12 minutes or until al dente, stirring occasionally to prevent sticking. Drain well. Divide among 6 warmed pasta bowls or plates.

4. Stir the pesto or basil into the sauce and correct the seasoning; discard the bay leaf. Ladle the sauce over the pasta. Top with the Parmesan cheese or pass it at the table.

*For a fine texture reminiscent of a Bolognese sauce, purée the sauce in a food processor at this point.

*Spaghetti and Zinfandel might be the quintessential American food and wine match. It is interesting to note that both are assumed to have an Italian heritage, but they have been transformed by our climate and our culture. This is a classic recipe that required one important change to make it work well with the wine, and that is the substitution of red bell pepper for the overly vegetal green. I also sometimes omit the tomato paste for a meatier-flavored sauce. Either way is fine with the wine.*

Serves Six

Often a dish with simple, straightforward flavors is the best accompaniment to a good bottle of wine. This simple cheese and tomato pizza is a case in point, allowing the complex flavors in a really good Zinfandel to shine. Although fontina cheese is made in many countries, those from Italy or Argentina have more depth of flavor to match the strength of a Zinfandel. Roasting the tomatoes also produces more intense flavors, and is truly worth the extra effort.

Yields One Twelve-Inch Pizza

# ROASTED TOMATO AND FONTINA PIZZA

4 Roma tomatoes
olive oil
salt and freshly ground black pepper
dough for 1 (12-inch) pizza (page 62)
cornmeal
2 ounces fontina cheese, shredded
2 tablespoons freshly grated Parmesan cheese
1 tablespoon chopped fresh oregano

1. Preheat the oven to 350 degrees. Cut the tomatoes into 3/8-inch slices, discarding the stem ends. Arrange the slices in an oiled baking pan. Brush the tops with olive oil and sprinkle with salt and pepper. Roast for 30 minutes. Turn the slices over and season again. Roast for 30 minutes longer or until the slices begin to color. Cool in the baking pan.

2. Place a pizza stone or unglazed paving tile on the lowest rack of an electric oven or directly on the floor of a gas oven. Increase the oven temperature to 450 degrees. Heat for 30 minutes or longer.

3. Stretch or roll the pizza dough to a 12-inch circle on a floured surface. Place on the back of a baking sheet or a pizza peel sprinkled with cornmeal. Brush the dough with olive oil. Sprinkle with the fontina cheese and arrange the tomato slices over the top.

4. Shake the pan or peel sharply to loosen the pizza and slide it onto the hot pizza stone. Bake for 10 minutes or until the cheese melts and the crust is light brown. Sprinkle with the oregano. Cut into 6 wedges and serve immediately.

# Polenta Lasagna

4 cups water
1 teaspoon salt
1/2 teaspoon freshly ground black pepper
1 cup polenta
1 small onion, chopped
1 clove of garlic, minced
1/4 cup olive oil
2 pounds tomatoes, peeled, seeded, chopped, or
1 (28-ounce) can tomatoes with juice
1 tablespoon tomato paste
1 small bay leaf
1 teaspoon dried oregano
salt and pepper to taste
4 ounces Asiago cheese, grated
3/4 cup heavy cream
6 sprigs of fresh oregano for garnish

1. For the polenta, bring the water to a boil in a saucepan and add 1 teaspoon salt and 1/2 teaspoon pepper. Stir in the polenta. Reduce the heat and cook for 45 minutes or until the mixture begins to leave the side of the saucepan, stirring occasionally. Spread 1/2 inch thick in a 10x15-inch pan. Chill in the refrigerator.

2. For the sauce, sauté the onion and garlic in the heated olive oil in a medium saucepan over medium heat until translucent. Add the tomatoes, tomato paste, bay leaf and oregano. Cook for 20 to 30 minutes or until of the desired consistency. Season with salt and pepper to taste.* Discard the bay leaf.

3. For the lasagna, preheat the oven to 350 degrees. Spread the sauce in a large baking dish. Cut the polenta into triangles. Arrange in the prepared baking dish in an overlapping layer with the points on top. Sprinkle with the cheese. Pour the cream over the top.

4. Bake for 40 to 45 minutes. Let stand for several minutes. Cut into 6 portions. Serve on warmed plates, garnished with sprigs of fresh oregano.

*Add 1 to 2 teaspoons sugar to the sauce if the tomatoes are out of season or if using canned tomatoes.

*Polenta gets just enough sweetness from corn to make it a problem for most red wines. Zinfandel, with all its berry fruit and spice, handles it easily. Those same qualities in the wine also make the best match to tomato sauces, with the fruit in the wine aligning with that of the tomato, and the spiciness balancing the acid.*

Serves Six

*This can be a great vegetarian dish for Zinfandel. The fruit of the tomato is matched by the fruity character of the wine, while the black olives provide the depth and flavor intensity to balance the power of the red wine. If you have a lighter, fruitier style of Zinfandel, use a mild olive. If you have a Cabernet wanna-be powerhouse-style Zinfandel, go for the earthy oil-cured olive.*

Serves Four to Six

# TOMATO AND BLACK OLIVE RISOTTO

1 small onion, chopped
1 to 2 tablespoons olive oil
2 cloves garlic, minced
1½ cups uncooked Arborio rice
1 pound fresh tomatoes, peeled, chopped, or
1 (14-ounce) can chopped tomatoes
16 to 24 black olives, pitted, slivered*
4 to 5 cups chicken stock or vegetable stock or
1 (14-ounce) can stock diluted with water
salt and freshly ground black pepper
4 basil leaves
freshly grated Parmesan cheese and
basil sprigs for garnish

1. Sauté the onion in the heated olive oil in a wide heavy saucepan for 3 minutes or until translucent. Stir in the garlic and rice, coating well. Add the fresh tomatoes or undrained canned tomatoes and olives and mix well.

2. Bring the chicken stock to a simmer over medium heat. Add enough of the hot stock to just cover the rice in a saucepan and adjust the heat so the mixture bubbles gently. Ladle in enough additional stock to cover the rice as the stock is absorbed. Begin to taste-test the rice when the liquid begins to thicken and cook just until the rice is tender. Remove from the heat and season with salt and pepper.

3. Cut the basil leaves into thin shreds. Add to the risotto. Serve immediately in warmed soup plates. Garnish with Parmesan cheese and basil sprigs.

*Add the lesser amount of olives if you are using a type with a strong flavor, such as oil-cured.

# CIOPPINO

2 onions, chopped
2 red bell peppers, seeded, chopped
1/4 cup olive oil
4 cloves of garlic, minced
1 bay leaf
1/2 teaspoon dried oregano
1/2 teaspoon paprika
4 pounds tomatoes, peeled, chopped, or
2 (28-ounce) cans tomatoes with juice
1 1/2 cups Zinfandel
2 (8-ounce) bottles clam juice
salt and freshly ground black pepper to taste
2 pounds fresh fish, such as cod, red snapper,
rockfish, halibut, crab meat or shrimp
best quality olive oil
2 tablespoons chopped fresh Italian parsley,
oregano and/or basil

1. Sauté the onions and red bell peppers in 1/4 cup heated olive oil in a wide heavy saucepan over medium heat for 2 to 3 minutes, stirring occasionally. Add the garlic, bay leaf, oregano and paprika and cook for 5 minutes longer.

2. Add the tomatoes, wine and clam juice. Simmer for 15 minutes or until the vegetables are tender, adding additional water as needed for a soupy consistency. Season with salt and pepper.

3. Cut the fish into serving pieces and place gently in the sauce. Bring to a simmer and simmer for 5 to 10 minutes or until the fish is firm or until cooked crab meat is heated through.

4. Transfer the fish to warmed soup plates. Ladle the sauce around the fish, discarding the bay leaf. Garnish with a drizzle of olive oil and sprinkle with the fresh herbs. Serve immediately.

*Cioppino is a tomato-based seafood stew that was created by Italian fishermen in San Francisco around the turn of the century. Today, Dungeness crab is considered a required ingredient, but I like the early fisherman's tradition of using whatever is freshest. No matter what seafood you choose, it is the tomato base which ties the dish to Zinfandel. Note that green bell pepper is not used, as its strong vegetal character interferes with the fruit in the wine.*

Serves Four to Six

*Balsamic vinegar is concentrated by aging it in various kinds of wood barrels. The resulting flavor is too sweet for many red wines, but Zinfandel has the fruitiness to handle it.*

Serves Four

———

# CHICKEN BRAISED IN BALSAMIC VINEGAR

1 (3- to 4- pound) frying chicken, cut into 8 pieces
salt and freshly ground black pepper to taste
2 tablespoons olive oil
2 slices bacon, cut into 1/4-inch pieces
1 onion, chopped
4 large shallots, split into halves
4 carrots, cut into 3/4-inch pieces
2 cloves of garlic, minced
1 tablespoon flour
1/2 cup chicken stock
1/4 cup balsamic vinegar
3/4 cup Zinfandel
1 bay leaf
2 tablespoons chopped Italian parsley for garnish

1. Preheat the oven to 325 degrees. Rinse the chicken and pat dry; season with salt and pepper. Brown in the heated olive oil in a 10- to 12-inch Dutch oven or oven-proof skillet. Remove the chicken to a dish and drain all but 2 tablespoons of the drippings from the Dutch oven.

2. Add the bacon, onion, shallots, carrots and garlic. Cook for 3 minutes or until the onion begins to become tender, stirring constantly. Sprinkle with the flour and mix well. Stir in the chicken stock, vinegar, wine and bay leaf. Add all the chicken pieces but the breast pieces.

3. Braise, covered, in the oven for 30 minutes. Season with salt and pepper and add the chicken breast pieces. Braise, uncovered, for 20 minutes longer. Serve over rice or egg noodles, discarding the bay leaf; garnish with the parsley.

# MARY'S BARBECUED SPARERIBS

1/2 cup olive oil
1/2 cup Zinfandel
1/3 cup tomato paste
1 tablespoon brown sugar
1/2 to 1 teaspoon Tabasco sauce
2 large cloves garlic, minced
1 teaspoon paprika
1 bay leaf, crumbled
1 teaspoon salt
4 to 5 pounds pork spareribs

**1.** Whisk the olive oil, wine, tomato paste, brown sugar, Tabasco sauce, garlic, paprika, bay leaf and salt together in a very large bowl.

**2.** To strip the tough membrane from the back of the ribs, hold a fork upright with the tines facing you. Rake the fork toward the meatier side of the rack, moving parallel to the bones. Cut the ribs apart in 1- to 4-rib sections. Add to the sauce, coating well. Marinate in the refrigerator for 2 to 24 hours.

**3.** Preheat the oven to 350 degrees. Place the ribs on racks over a pan with 1/2 inch of water. Roast for 1 1/2 to 2 hours. You may roast for 1 hour and finish on the grill if preferred.

---

*Barbecue is an American institution. The combination of Zinfandel and barbecue is the standard in California. It stands to reason, as Zinfandel has the fruit to match that of the tomato-based sauces and the spice to stand up to a little bit of heat.*

Serves Four to Six

*Bump up the brown sugar and Tabasco sauce and you move this dish to a fruity blush wine that can handle the higher levels of sweet and hot. If you are going for a Texas-style, really HOT sauce, you'll do better to switch to beer.*

CABERNET

Cabernet Sauvignon, Merlot, and Meritage are the best loved of full bodied red wines. Cabernet Sauvignon grapes are much more widely planted than any other fine wine grape variety and, in Bordeaux, have traditionally been blended with varying amounts of Merlot, Cabernet Franc, and/or Petit Verdot. Some California producers have joined together and coined the term "Meritage" to name these blends. This allows them to make the best blend they can without concern about percentages, and it also identifies the wine as being in a style similar to those in Bordeaux. Although each of these varieties has its own particular profile, in general they tend to have the same relationship with food.

Young Cabernets, Merlots, and Meritage varieties are intensely colored and flavored, with a pronounced structure created by the tannins that come from the seeds and skins of the grape. As they age, the acids and tannins soften, resulting in a much more subtle wine. Look for softer food flavors if you have the opportunity to enjoy one of these older vintages.

# S A U V I G N O N

## CHAMELEON RECIPES

## CABERNET SAUVIGNON RECIPES

# CABERNET SAUVIGNON PROFILE

## Food Affinities

| SEAFOOD | MEAT & POULTRY | HERBS & SPICES | SAUCES | CHEESE & NUTS | VEGETABLES & FRUITS |
|---|---|---|---|---|---|
| halibut | bacon | black pepper | meat stock | aged goat | Belgian endive |
| rare tuna | beef | garlic | reduction | cheese | black |
| salmon | duck | juniper | red wine | aged provolone | chanterelles |
| | foie gras | lavender | soy | cheese | carrots |
| | lamb | mustard | walnut | blue cheese | eggplant |
| | sausage | rosemary | | Camembert | lentils |
| | squab | savory | | cheese | morels |
| | wild game | star anise | | Parmesan | oil-cured olives |
| | | Szechuan | | cheese | radicchio |
| | | pepper | | sharp Cheddar | red chard |
| | | thyme | | cheese | summer squash |
| | | | | walnuts | wild rice |

## Food Conflicts

| SEAFOOD | MEAT & POULTRY | HERBS & SPICES | SAUCES | CHEESE & NUTS | VEGETABLES & FRUITS |
|---|---|---|---|---|---|
| oysters | pheasant | chilies | citrus | cream cheese | asparagus |
| smoked fish | pork | cilantro | cream | Jack cheese | corn/polenta |
| sole | veal | cumin | vinegar | Swiss cheese | green beans |
| | | | | unripe Brie | most fruit |
| | | | | cheese | snow peas |

### Wine Flavors:
Black currant, cassis, tea, eucalyptus, mint, chocolate, cedar, tobacco

### Wine Textures:
Tannic/bitter, acidic

### Complementary Cuisines:
Simpler preparations from France, Italy, or the Northern United States are suited to the complexities of Cabernet Sauvignon.

### Best Methods of Preparation:
Grilling, roasting, braising

### Ideal Occasions:
Formal dinners are ideal occasions to break out well-aged, fine old wines. Serve the young ones at a winter grill or ski weekend.

In Tuscany, this soup is known as Ribollita because the beans are cooked twice. I like this version even better (Trebollita?) in which the soup is baked in the oven with thick slices of red onion on top. This is a hearty, stick-to-your-ribs winter dish that can easily match the power of the most intense Cabernet. The use of rosemary, which is a member of the mint family, highlights the eucalyptus/mint flavors often found in this wine.

Serves Eight

# TUSCAN BEAN AND CABBAGE SOUP

4 large red onions
3 cloves garlic
¾ cup extra-virgin olive oil
1 rib celery with leaves, chopped
1 carrot, peeled, chopped
1 leek, chopped
1 tomato, chopped
1 pound dried Great Northern beans or cannellini
2 thick slices prosciutto, chopped
2½ quarts water
1 pound red cabbage, coarsely chopped
1 sprig rosemary
1 sprig thyme
salt and freshly ground black pepper to taste
8 thick slices Italian bread
¾ cup grated Parmesan cheese

1. Chop 2 of the onions and ½ clove of the garlic. Sauté in ¼ cup of the olive oil in a heavy ovenproof Dutch oven. Add the celery, carrot, leek and tomato. Sauté until the vegetables are light brown.

2. Rinse and sort the beans. Add to the Dutch oven with the prosciutto and water. Cook over medium heat for about 1 hour or until the beans are tender, stirring occasionally.

3. Remove ½ cup of the beans and purée in a blender or food processor. Return to the Dutch oven with the cabbage. Simmer during remaining preparation time.

4. Crush the remaining 2½ cloves of garlic. Sauté with the rosemary and thyme in ¼ cup of the olive oil in a sauté pan. Add to the soup and season with salt and pepper.

5. Preheat the oven to 350 degrees. Cut the remaining 2 onions into thick slices. Arrange on top of the soup. Drizzle with the remaining ¼ cup olive oil. Bake for 30 minutes or until the onions are golden brown.

6. Place 1 slice of bread in each soup bowl. Ladle the soup over the bread and place 1 onion slice on each serving. Sprinkle with the cheese or pass it at the table.

# DUCK AND WILD RICE SALAD WITH TOASTED WALNUT VINAIGRETTE

2 whole boned duck breasts with skin
1/2 cup water    salt to taste
1 cup uncooked wild rice    3 1/2 cups water
1 teaspoon salt    3 green onions with tops, sliced
2 ounces radicchio, thinly shredded
1/4 cup coarsely chopped toasted walnuts
2 tablespoons walnut oil
2 teaspoons sherry wine vinegar
freshly ground black pepper to taste    2 Belgian endive

1. For the cracklings, rinse the duck breasts and pat dry. Remove the skin with the fat from the duck and cut the skin into small pieces.* Combine the skin with 1/2 cup water in a heavy skillet. Cook over medium heat for 45 to 60 minutes or until the fat is totally rendered and the skin is golden brown, stirring occasionally. Drain the skin cracklings on paper towels and sprinkle lightly with salt to taste. Reserve the rendered fat for another use.

2. Rinse the wild rice in cold water and combine with 3 1/2 cups water and 1 teaspoon salt in a saucepan. Bring to a boil and reduce the heat. Simmer, covered, for 45 minutes or until the rice kernels begin to split open. Drain and place in a large bowl to cool.

3. Add the green onions, radicchio and walnuts to the cooled rice. Add the walnut oil and vinegar and toss to coat well. Season with salt and pepper to taste.

4. Season the duck breasts with salt and pepper to taste. Grill or sauté for 3 minutes on each side. Let stand for 5 minutes. Slice on the diagonal. Reserve the 16 best slices; chop the remaining duck.

5. Separate 12 endive leaves from the heads. Cut the remaining endive into thin slices and add to the rice; toss to mix well.

6. Arrange 3 endive leaves and 4 duck slices on each serving plate. Spoon the rice salad into the center. Top with the duck skin cracklings and a fresh grinding of pepper to taste.

*The duck skin will be easier to chop if it is first spread on baking sheets and partially frozen.

*This is a perfect entrée salad to serve in the summer when you want to enjoy a Cabernet or Merlot, but you don't feel like eating a heavy meal. Although light on the palate, this dish gets plenty of power from the tannins in the walnuts and walnut oil, the deep earthy flavor of the wild rice, and the richness of the duck—all qualities found in the wine.*

Serves Four

Serves Six

# LENTIL AND RADICCHIO SALAD WITH GOAT CHEESE AND PANCETTA

4 thick slices pancetta, diced
1 carrot, chopped
1 small onion, chopped
1 rib celery, chopped
1 cup uncooked lentils, preferably French green lentils
1 head radicchio
1 teaspoon Dijon mustard
1 tablespoon balsamic vinegar
1/3 cup olive oil
salt and freshly ground black pepper to taste
4 to 6 ounces aged goat cheese, cut into 6 small rounds
fresh thyme leaves for garnish

1. Sauté the pancetta in a heavy saucepan until brown. Remove with a slotted spoon and drain on paper towels.

2. Add the carrot, onion and celery to the drippings in the saucepan. Sauté for 2 to 3 minutes, stirring occasionally. Add the lentils and water to cover. Simmer for 20 to 25 minutes or until the lentils are tender; drain.

3. Remove 6 outer leaves of the radicchio carefully to form serving cups for the salad. Shred the remaining radicchio.

4. Whisk the Dijon mustard, vinegar and olive oil together in a bowl. Add the lentils and shredded radicchio and toss to coat well. Season with salt and pepper.

5. Place the radicchio-leaf cups on the serving plates. Spoon the lentil mixture into the cups. Top with the goat cheese and sprinkle with the pancetta. Finish with a final grind of pepper and garnish with thyme leaves.

# STEAK SALAD WITH BLUE CHEESE DRESSING

1 or 2 large onions, thinly sliced
flour
salt and freshly ground black pepper to taste
vegetable oil for deep-frying
2 (12-ounce) New York steaks, trimmed
4 ounces blue cheese
1 cup light sour cream
1 tablespoon white wine vinegar
2 tablespoons chopped chives
12 cups salad greens with arugula and watercress
chives for garnish

1. For the onion rings, separate the onion slices into rings Toss with a mixture of flour, salt and pepper to taste. Preheat the oil to 375 degrees in a deep-fryer. Add the onion rings in small batches and deep-fry until light brown. Spread on paper towels to drain; salt lightly. Place in a warm oven to crisp while preparing the salad.

2. For the steaks, preheat the grill or broiler. Sprinkle the steaks with salt and pepper. Grill for 5 minutes on each side for rare. Let stand for 5 minutes or longer.

3. For the dressing, combine the blue cheese, sour cream, vinegar and 2 tablespoons chives in a food processor. Process until smooth.

4. For the salad, wash and dry the salad greens. Divide among 4 or 6 serving plates. Slice the steak and arrange on the plate. Top with the dressing and fried onion rings. Garnish with additional chives.

*A big, powerful wine like Cabernet requires formidable flavors to stand up to it. Steak and blue cheese definitely qualify. If you are trying to watch your fat intake, skip the deep-fried onions, serve a smaller portion of meat, and use nonfat sour cream in the dressing. To replace the crunch of the fried onions, toast slices or cubes of onion bread in a 300-degree oven for twenty minutes or until they are crisp and golden brown.*

Serves Four to Six

Even though tomatoes are the primary
ingredient, this dish is driven by the
stronger olive flavors. The earthy,
slightly bitter oil-cured olives call for a
Cabernet or Merlot, mirroring those
flavors in the wine.

Serves Four

This can be made into a Sauvignon
Blanc dish by substituting briny
kalamata olives, or one for Chardonnay
by using fat ripe green olives—
a really interesting exercise in food
and wine pairing.

# PASTA WITH MARINATED TOMATO SAUCE

2 pounds vine-ripened tomatoes in a variety of
sizes and colors if available
1/2 cup virgin olive oil
2 cloves garlic, minced
1/2 cup slivered pitted oil-cured olives
2 to 3 tablespoons coarsely chopped fresh basil leaves
salt and freshly ground black pepper to taste
1 pound uncooked spaghetti
4 basil sprigs for garnish

1. For the sauce, core the
tomatoes and squeeze out the seeds. Cut larger tomatoes into wedges
and smaller tomatoes into halves or quarters.

2. Toss the tomatoes with the
olive oil in a noncorrosive bowl. Add the garlic, olives and chopped
basil and season lightly with salt and pepper. Marinate for 2 hours.

3. Cook the pasta al dente using
the package directions; drain well. Add to the sauce and toss to coat
well. Garnish with basil sprigs and serve immediately.

# FETTUCINI WITH BRAISED DUCK SAUCE AND CRACKLINGS

6 duck legs with skin    1 cup water    salt to taste
3 cups chicken stock or duck stock
1 ounce dried porcini mushrooms
1 large red or yellow onion, thinly sliced
2 red bell peppers, seeded, julienned
1/4 cup olive oil    3 cloves garlic, minced
3 large tomatoes, seeded, chopped
2 small yellow squash, thinly sliced
2 small zucchini, thinly sliced
3 carrots, cut into thin strips
3 tablespoons mixed minced fresh oregano and thyme
freshly ground black pepper to taste
1 1/4 pounds uncooked fettucini
sprigs of oregano and thyme for garnish

1.    For the cracklings, remove the skin from the duck and chop the skin coarsely.* Combine with the water in a heavy skillet. Bring to a boil and reduce the heat. Simmer for about 1 hour or until the cracklings are golden brown, stirring occasionally. Remove with a slotted spoon and drain on paper towels. Season lightly with salt to taste.

2.    For the duck sauce, rinse the duck and pat dry. Combine with the stock in a saucepan. Bring to a boil and reduce the heat. Simmer for 1 hour or until tender. Remove the duck from the stock with a slotted spoon. Remove and discard the bones. Add the dried mushrooms to the hot stock. Simmer for 15 minutes. Remove the mushrooms, pressing to remove liquid. Mince the mushrooms. Strain the stock through a cheesecloth-lined strainer and return to the saucepan; keep warm.

3.    Sauté the onion, bell peppers and mushrooms in the heated olive oil in a large sauté pan for 3 minutes, stirring occasionally. Add the stock, garlic and tomatoes. Boil for 5 minutes. Add the duck meat, yellow squash, zucchini, carrots and minced herbs. Simmer for 2 to 3 minutes longer. Season with salt and pepper to taste.

4.    Cook the fettucini al dente in boiling salted water in a saucepan; drain. Toss with the duck sauce in a bowl. Sprinkle with the cracklings. Garnish with herb sprigs.

*The duck skin will be easier to chop if it is first spread on baking sheets and partially frozen.

*Even though there are a lot of vegetables in this sauce, the rich unctuousness of the braised duck takes precedence on the palate. This makes a perfect foil for the power of a Cabernet or Merlot. Rendering the skin into crisp cracklings augments the pairing while adding a nice textural contrast.*

Serves Six

The main vehicle for this pairing is the fat—of the olives, the cheese, and the butter in the pastry. This coats the palate, making the tannic aspects of a young Cabernet seem softer. Oil-cured olives have an earthy, slightly bitter flavor which aligns with those flavors in the wine. They may be substituted for part of the olives in this recipe, but they are strong in flavor, so I would suggest using them only for one-fourth to one-third of the total amount.

Yields 16 Pizette

# BLACK OLIVE PESTO PIZETTE

2 cloves garlic, peeled
2 tablespoons pine nuts
1/2 cup olive oil
3/4 cup freshly grated Asiago or Parmesan cheese
2 cans pitted black olives, drained
1 (2-sheet) package frozen puff pastry, thawed

1. For the olive pesto, process the garlic and pine nuts in a food processor fitted with a steel blade until finely chopped. Add the olive oil, cheese and half the olives; process until smooth. Slice the remaining olives and combine with the puréed mixture in a bowl.

2. Preheat the oven to 450 degrees. Cut the puff pastry into 16 rounds. Place on a lightly greased baking sheet. Spread with the olive pesto.* Bake for 15 minutes or until the edges of the pastry are light brown.

*There will be olive pesto left over from this recipe. Use it on sandwiches, pasta, more pizette or a pizza made with basic pizza dough (page 62).

# TOMATO AND CHEESE PIE

1 recipe biscuit dough (proportions for 2 cups flour)
6 large ripe tomatoes
2 tablespoons chopped fresh basil
1 teaspoon salt
1/2 teaspoon freshly ground black pepper
1 cup shredded sharp Cheddar cheese
3/4 cup sour cream
3/4 cup mayonnaise

1. Preheat the oven to 400 degrees. Line a buttered quiche or pie dish with the biscuit dough.

2. Seed, juice and coarsely chop the tomatoes. Mix with the basil, salt and pepper in a bowl. Spoon into the prepared pie shell.

3. Combine the cheese, sour cream and mayonnaise in a bowl and mix well. Spread over the filling. Bake for 15 minutes. Reduce the oven temperature to 350 degrees. Bake for 20 minutes longer or until the top is browned.

*I first found this old American recipe in James Beard's American Cooking. I have made revisions to effect a more successful pairing with Cabernet Sauvignon or Merlot. Fresh tomatoes are often too acidic for these wines, making them taste heavy and bitter. In this recipe, the fat of the mayonnaise, cheese, and sour cream predominate, softening the effects of the acid in the tomatoes.*

Serves Six

*A milder cheese such as Monterey Jack or fontina would take this dish to Chardonnay.*

*Lentils have an earthy flavor which matches that in Cabernet Sauvignon or Merlot. The match is bolstered by the richness of the chicken stock and bacon. Although sun-dried tomatoes have a concentration of fruit sugars, they are dispersed by the cooking method, so there is no conflict with the wine.*

Serves Four to Six

——

# BRAISED LENTILS WITH SUN-DRIED TOMATOES

1 1/2 ounces sun-dried tomatoes
3 slices pancetta or bacon, cut into 1/4-inch pieces
1 small clove garlic, minced
1 small onion, chopped
2 ribs celery, chopped
2 carrots, peeled, chopped
1 cup dried lentils*
3 cups low-salt chicken stock or unsalted chicken stock
1 tablespoon balsamic vinegar
1/3 cup chopped fresh parsley
salt and freshly ground black pepper to taste

1. Soak the sun-dried tomatoes in hot water in a bowl for 20 minutes. Drain and chop.

2. Cook the pancetta in a heavy saucepan over medium heat until it begins to brown. Add the garlic, onion, celery and carrots. Sauté for 3 minutes.

3. Add the tomatoes, lentils, chicken stock and vinegar to the saucepan. Bring to a boil and reduce the heat. Simmer, partially covered, for 15 minutes. Increase the heat.

4. Cook, uncovered, for 15 minutes longer or just until the lentils are tender; the mixture should be thick and most of the liquid absorbed. Stir in the parsley and season with salt and pepper to taste. Serve immediately.

*French *lentilles de Puy* are visually more attractive than domestic lentils. They are a pretty dark grey-green and hold their shape better. Domestic lentils, however, will taste just as good.

# WILD RICE RISOTTO

1/2 cup uncooked wild rice
2 cups cold water
1 teaspoon salt
1 small red onion, chopped
3 tablespoons olive oil
2 medium carrots, peeled, chopped
1 clove garlic, minced
1 cup uncooked Arborio rice
1/2 cup Cabernet Sauvignon
4 to 5 cups duck stock or chicken stock
2 medium beets, parboiled, peeled, chopped
salt and freshly ground black pepper to taste
1/2 cup coarsely chopped Italian parsley and/or
1/2 cup freshly grated Parmesan cheese for garnish

1. Combine the wild rice with the cold water and 1 teaspoon salt in a saucepan. Simmer, covered, for 30 to 40 minutes or just until the kernels begin to split; drain well.

2. Sauté the onion briefly in the heated olive oil in a heavy wide-bottomed saucepan. Add the carrots and garlic. Sauté for 2 to 3 minutes. Add the Arborio rice and wild rice and mix to coat well. Add the Cabernet. Cook until the wine has nearly evaporated, stirring constantly.

3. Bring the duck stock to a simmer in a saucepan and maintain at a simmer. Add just enough of the heated stock at a time to cover the rice, maintaining a simmer. Add the beets and continue to simmer. Continue to add the stock and simmer until the rice is tender.* Season with salt and pepper to taste. Serve immediately. Garnish with the parsley and cheese.

*It may not be necessary to add all of the stock, or it may be necessary to augment the amount of stock with water to finish cooking the rice.

*I love risotto. Its creaminess makes a nice balance with the acidity of wine. The addition of earthy wild rice and beets make a match here with the earthiness of a Cabernet Sauvignon or Merlot. Notice when boiling the wild rice that it gives off the aroma of black tea; this suggests to me that there may be some tannins in it as well, although I've never seen that written anywhere.*

Serves Six to Eight as a Side Dish
or
Four as an Entrée

I got this idea for grilling fish wrapped in fig leaves from Paul Bertolli's book for Chez Panisse. The char of the grilled leaves combined with the fat richness of salmon makes a fish dish that is really wonderful with red wine. Cabernet is singled out by using it in a reduction sauce. Grilling the vegetables gives them a depth of flavor that also suits the intensity of Cabernet.

Serves Six

By substituting the Pinot Noir Sauce on page 108, this dish would be equally enjoyable with Pinot Noir.

# SALMON GRILLED IN FIG LEAVES

6 large fig leaves
olive oil
2 pounds salmon fillets, 1 inch thick, cut into 6 pieces
salt and freshly ground black pepper to taste
3 medium boiling potatoes
2 Japanese eggplant
2 zucchini
3 cups Cabernet Sauvignon
1 tablespoon cassis syrup or crème de cassis
½ cup demi-glace
chives for garnish

1. Wash and stem the fig leaves. Brush the dull side generously with olive oil. Brush the salmon fillets with olive oil and season with salt and pepper. Wrap the salmon in the fig leaves with the shiny side out. Set aside.

2. Boil the potatoes in salted water in a saucepan just until tender. Cool and cut crosswise into halves. Cut a slice off the ends of the pieces so they will stand.

3. Cut the eggplant and zucchini into ½-inch slices. Combine with the potatoes and a small amount of olive oil in a bowl. Season with salt and pepper.

4. For the wine sauce, heat the Cabernet and cassis syrup in a nonreactive saucepan until reduced to 1 cup. Stir in the demi-glace. Season with salt and pepper and keep warm.

5. Preheat a gas grill or prepare a charcoal fire. Place the salmon packages fold side down on the grill. Grill for 4 minutes on each side or just until the fish is firm. Grill the vegetables for 1 to 2 minutes on each side or just until tender.

6. Spoon the wine sauce onto 6 warmed plates. Cut the salmon packages into halves and arrange on the plates. Arrange the vegetables on the plates, standing the potatoes. Garnish with chives and serve immediately.

# TUNA WITH LAVENDER

3 cups Cabernet Sauvignon or Merlot
1 tablespoon cassis syrup or crème de cassis
½ cup demi-glace
salt to taste
2 tablespoons whole black peppercorns
2 tablespoons Szechuan peppercorns*
2 to 4 tablespoons dried lavender flowers and/or buds
2 pounds fresh tuna, cut into thick pieces
3 tablespoons olive oil
fresh lavender flowers for garnish

1. For the sauce, combine the Cabernet Sauvignon and cassis syrup in a nonreactive saucepan. Cook until reduced to about 1 cup. Add the demi-glace and simmer until the sauce has thickened. Adjust the seasoning and keep warm.

2. For the lavender-pepper, crush the black peppercorns and Szechuan peppercorns with a pestle, spice grinder or the steel blade of a food processor. Add the dried lavender and crush briefly in the same manner.

3. Press some of the lavender-pepper onto both sides of the tuna slices, reserving the remainder for another use. Salt the tuna lightly. Sear in the olive oil in a sauté pan over high heat for 1 to 2 minutes on each side for rare; check for desired doneness by piercing with the point of a small sharp knife.

4. Slice the tuna to show the rare center. Spoon the sauce onto 6 serving plates. Add the tuna slices and garnish with fresh lavender flowers. Serve with garlic mashed potatoes, baby beets and/or turnips.

*Szechuan peppercorns are available at Asian markets.

**Dried lavender is available in many health food stores. The intensity of flavor can, however, vary considerably. If the aroma is very faint, add more to the mix. If it is home-dried and very strong, use the lesser amount.

*I thought of using lavender with a Cabernet dish when I found out it was in the mint family, as is rosemary. Fresh tuna, when served rare, has the palate impression of beef, with dark meaty flavors. The black pepper has a taming effect on the intense tannins of Cabernet and Merlot, releasing more fruit flavors in the wine.*

Serves Six

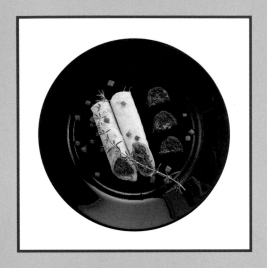

Soy sauce, I have discovered, has a great affinity for wine. One reason is the salt content, which works in balance with the acid base of wine. I also suspect that the fact that both wine and soy sauce are fermented creates additional affinity. The bit of sweetness from the ginger and sun-dried tomatoes is reined in by the pungency of the thyme and rosemary, but a softer, fruitier style of Cabernet or Merlot will be best with this dish.

Serves Six to Eight
___

# DUCK TORTILLAS

2 (5- to 6-pound) ducks, cut into quarters
1 cup water
salt to taste
3 cups low-salt chicken stock or unsalted chicken stock
1 teaspoon chopped fresh ginger
2 tablespoons sun-dried tomatoes
2 tablespoons rice wine or dry sherry
3 tablespoons soy sauce
3 tablespoons plum sauce or plum jam
1 tablespoon fresh thyme leaves
2 sprigs fresh rosemary
16 small flour tortillas
rehydrated sun-dried tomatoes and rosemary sprigs for garnish

1. For the cracklings, remove the skin from the breasts and thighs of the ducks. Place the skin in the freezer until partially frozen if time allows. Chop the skin coarsely. Combine with the water in a skillet. Cook over medium heat for 1 hour or until the fat has been rendered and the skin is golden brown. Drain the cracklings on paper towels and salt lightly; reserve the duck fat for another use.

2. Combine the chicken stock, ginger, 2 tablespoons sun-dried tomatoes, rice wine, soy sauce, plum sauce, thyme and 2 sprigs rosemary in a large saucepan. Bring to a simmer and add the duck. Simmer, covered, for 1 hour or until the duck meat falls from the bones.

3. Cool the duck in the stock.* Remove and chop the meat, discarding the bones. Strain the stock and skim the fat. Cook the stock until reduced to about 1 cup. Add the duck and reheat.

4. Preheat the oven to 325 degrees. Wrap the tortillas in foil. Heat in the oven for 10 to 15 minutes.

5. Spoon the duck mixture onto the warmed tortillas. Roll the tortillas to enclose the filling. Sprinkle with the cracklings. Garnish with sun-dried tomatoes and additonal rosemary sprigs.

*Chill the stock overnight for easy removal of the fat. The dish does not suffer with reheating.

# GRILLED DUCK BREASTS WITH CABERNET SAUCE

6 to 8 boned duck breast halves
1 cup water
salt to taste
3 cups Cabernet Sauvignon
1 tablespoon cassis syrup or crème de cassis
¹/₂ cup duck and veal demi-glace
freshly ground black pepper to taste
1 teaspoon chopped fresh rosemary

**1.** For the cracklings, remove the skin from the duck breasts. Place the skin in the freezer until partially frozen if time allows. Chop coarsely. Combine with the water in a heavy skillet. Simmer over medium-low heat until all the fat has been rendered and the skin is golden brown. Drain the cracklings on paper towels and salt lightly; reserve the duck fat for another use.

**2.** For the Cabernet sauce, cook the wine with the cassis syrup in a nonreactive saucepan until reduced to 1 cup. Stir in the demi-glace. Season with salt and pepper to taste and keep warm.

**3.** Preheat the grill. Season the duck with the rosemary and salt and pepper to taste. Grill for 3 to 4 minutes on each side for rare.

**4.** Spoon the sauce onto the serving plates. Slice the duck and fan over the sauce. Sprinkle with the cracklings. Serve with wild rice risotto (page 141) or roasted vegetables chosen from the list on the profile page (page 131).

*The rich deep flavors of duck are compatible with many red wines. In this case, the pairing is made intentionally by the use of a reduction sauce of the wine of choice, Cabernet Sauvignon. The minty flavors of the rosemary and the black currant of the cassis also align particularly well with similar flavors in Cabernet.*

Serves Six to Eight
━━━━

*Squab is the darkest of all-dark-meat birds, the perfect accompaniment to deep dark Cabernet Sauvignon. If squab is not available, substitute duck breast in this recipe; the pairing is based on the fat balancing the tannins in the wine. Cabbage is a wine-friendly vegetable, the red having a little bit of sweetness. This is balanced by the addition of acid with the balsamic vinegar and the saltiness of the bacon. I like to hide some creamy mashed potatoes under the braised cabbage; it makes a nice surprise for the diner and adds another complementary textural note to the dish.*

Serves Four to Six

# SQUAB WITH BRAISED CABBAGE

4 ounces thick-sliced bacon, cut into strips
2 tablespoons duck fat or olive oil
2 red onions, sliced
8 ounces carrots, peeled, julienned
8 ounces red cabbage, shredded
8 ounces green cabbage, shredded
8 ounces Napa or savoy cabbage, shredded
2 to 3 tablespoons balsamic vinegar
salt and freshly ground black pepper to taste
4 to 6 whole squab breasts
1 recipe Cabernet sauce (page 145)
1/4 cup chopped Italian parsley
parsley leaves for garnish

1. For the cabbage, cook the bacon in a large heavy saucepan until crisp. Remove to a paper towel with a slotted spoon to drain, reserving the drippings. Add the duck fat to the drippings. Add the onions and sauté for 3 minutes. Add the carrots. Sauté until tender-crisp. Stir in all the cabbage. Sauté just until wilted. Add the balsamic vinegar and season with salt and pepper.

2. Season the squab with salt and pepper. Sear skin side down in an oiled skillet over medium-high heat for 2 to 3 minutes or until the skin is golden brown. Turn and brown on the other side, testing for doneness with the point of a sharp knife; do not cook beyond medium-rare or squab becomes tough and dry. Remove to a warm plate and tent with foil to keep warm.

3. Heat the Cabernet sauce to serving temperature. Reheat the cabbage; stir in the chopped parsley and adjust the seasonings. Slice the squab.

4. Spoon the sauce onto 1 side of each warmed serving plate. Arrange the squab slices in the sauce. Spoon the cabbage onto the plates, over a helping of mashed potatoes if desired. Garnish with parsley leaves and reserved bacon. Serve immediately.

# GRILLED SAUSAGE WITH RED ONION MARMALADE

4 red onions, thinly sliced
3 tablespoons unsalted butter
2 cups Cabernet Sauvignon
2 tablespoons crème de cassis, black currant liqueur, or cassis syrup
2 tablespoons balsamic vinegar
salt and freshly ground black pepper to taste
6 large baking potatoes
¼ cup olive oil or melted butter
8 large sweet Italian sausages, duck sausages or lamb sausages
fresh thyme leaves for garnish

1.  For the onion marmalade, cook the onions in the melted butter in a large heavy saucepan over low heat for up to 1 hour or until the onions are very tender, stirring occasionally. Increase the heat and add the Cabernet, crème de cassis and vinegar. Bring to a boil and reduce the heat. Simmer until all the liquid has been absorbed into the onions. Season with salt and pepper to taste.

2.  Peel the potatoes and cut into halves lengthwise. Cut each half into thin slices crosswise, holding the slices in place to retain the potato shape. Place on a baking sheet generously brushed with the olive oil or butter, pressing lightly to spread the slices slightly. Brush with additional olive oil or butter and sprinkle with salt and pepper.

3.  Preheat the oven to 400 degrees. Bake the potatoes for 30 minutes or until tender and browned on the edges, rotating the pan halfway though the cooking time for even browning.

4.  Preheat a gas grill or prepare a charcoal fire. Pierce sausages that are high in fat with a sharp knife and parboil for 2 to 3 minutes; drain. Grill until the sausages are firm to the touch and brown.

5.  Slice the sausages diagonally. Place a spoonful of the onion marmalade in the center of each serving plate. Arrange the potatoes and sausage slices around the marmalade in a propeller design. Serve immediately, garnished with a sprinkling of fresh thyme leaves.

*I have seen many recipes for onion marmalade that call for the addition of sugar. This results in a condiment that is so sweet that it makes any wine taste thin and sour. This version has a natural sweetness that develops from the long slow cooking of the onions, but it is held in balance by the acids of the wine and vinegar. The cassis provides a hint of black currant flavor that is also found in the Cabernet. Years ago, almost any sausage made would work with Cabernet. Today, with low-fat, Thai-flavored, southwestern spicy, etc., I recommend that you choose one of the sausages suggested in this recipe for the best pairing with Cabernet or Merlot.*

Serves Eight

Although I have heard people say that lamb and Pinot Noir is the classic match, I find that the strong lamb flavors are much better matched by the power of a great Cabernet or Merlot. All the other elements of this dish are harmonious with the lamb and the wine. This is a "company dish," for which I would choose the best Cabernet or Merlot I could find.

Serves Six

# RACK OF LAMB WITH SHALLOT MARMALADE AND CABERNET SAUCE

1 (7- to 8-pound) whole rack of lamb
3 cups Cabernet Sauvignon or Merlot    1 tablespoon cassis syrup
30 shallots    ¼ cup virgin olive oil
1 to 2 teaspoons balsamic vinegar
salt and freshly ground black pepper to taste
½ cup demi-glace    1 teaspoon chopped fresh rosemary
1 recipe white bean purée (page 149)    rosemary sprigs for garnish

1. Ask the butcher to prepare the rack of lamb by removing the chine bone and frenching the 2 sides; be sure he reserves the fat scraps.

2. Preheat the oven to 400 degrees. Trim any remaining fat from the lamb. Place all the fat scraps in a small roasting pan or cast-iron skillet. Roast for 2 hours or until brown, turning occasionally. Discard the fat scraps, reserving the pan drippings. Combine the Cabernet and cassis syrup in a nonreactive saucepan. Cook until reduced to about 1¼ cups. Set aside.

3. For the shallot marmalade, peel and finely chop 24 of the shallots. Sauté in the heated olive oil in a heavy saucepan over low heat until brown, stirring occasionally. Add 2 tablespoons of the wine reduction. Cook until all the liquid has evaporated. Set aside.

4. Cut the remaining 6 shallots into halves lengthwise. Steam for 3 minutes or just until tender; drain. Place cut side down in the reserved drippings in the roasting pan. Roast for 15 minutes or until brown on the bottom. Remove to a warmed plate. Add the roasted chopped shallots, balsamic vinegar, salt and pepper to the roasting pan. Keep warm.

5. For the sauce, add the demi-glace to the remaining wine reduction. Season with salt and pepper.

6. Preheat a gas grill or prepare a charcoal fire. Rub the lamb with olive oil and sprinkle with the chopped rosemary, salt and pepper. Grill for 10 to 12 minutes for rare, turning every 2 minutes. Let stand for 5 minutes; cut into chops. Pour any juices into the shallot marmalade.

7. Pipe white bean purée onto 6 warmed plates. Stand the chops against the purée and place 1 spoonful of the shallot marmalade in front of the chops. Spoon the sauce around the marmalade. Add 2 of the roasted shallot halves to each plate and garnish with rosemary sprigs. Serve immediately.

# WHITE BEAN PURÉE

16 ounces dried white beans
1 large onion, coarsely chopped
4 cloves garlic, peeled, crushed
2 tomatoes, peeled, coarsely chopped (optional)
4 cups vegetable stock, or 2 cups canned stock and 2 cups water
salt and freshly ground black pepper

**1.** Rinse and sort the beans. Combine with the onion, garlic, tomatoes and enough vegetable stock to cover in a deep saucepan. Bring to a boil and reduce the heat. Simmer for 1 hour or until the beans are tender, adding additional stock or water as needed to cover the beans.

**2.** Strain the beans, reserving the cooking liquid. Combine the beans with ⅓ cup of the cooking liquid in a food processor container. Process until the mixture holds its shape in a spoon, adding additional cooking liquid as needed. Season with salt and pepper to taste.

Note: Reheat the purée in the microwave or a double boiler, as it will stick to the pan if reheated on the stove top.

A *few years ago* I would have said that fat couldn't be removed from a cuisine that was meant to be served with wine, as the fat was necessary to balance the acid in the wine. Having researched low-fat cooking, I now know that there are some ingredients which can imitate fat on the palate. I place beans on the top of that list. I use this purée in place of mashed potatoes. The palate-coating aspect of the dish makes it an ideal accompaniment to astringent red wine. Leftovers are great spread on toasted or grilled bread.

Serves Eight to Ten

149

It is difficult to find dishes to match the intensity of Cabernet that aren't too heavy for summer dining. In this recipe, the ragout has plenty of deep rich flavors with absolutely no fat added. The red meat, char, and the fat of the filet are obvious matches with the Cabernet, but the ragout would also work with the wine as part of a vegetarian meal.

Serves Eight

# FILETS MIGNONS WITH BLACK BEAN RAGOUT

16 ounces dried black beans
4 or 5 leeks, white part only
1 large onion, chopped
2 cloves garlic, chopped
2 medium carrots, chopped
4 cups peeled, seeded, juiced, chopped tomatoes*
2 cups tomato juice*
1 tablespoon fresh thyme leaves, or 1 teaspoon dried thyme
¼ cup balsamic vinegar
salt and freshly ground black pepper to taste
vegetable oil for deep-frying
8 filets mignons, trimmed, tied
fresh thyme leaves and a variety of cherry tomatoes for garnish

1. For the ragout, rinse and sort the beans. Combine with cold water to cover in a saucepan. Cook, covered, until tender; drain well. Mash 1 cup of the beans.

2. Chop half the leeks. Combine the chopped leeks with the onion, garlic, carrots, half the tomatoes, tomato juice, thyme and mashed beans in a heavy saucepan. Simmer, uncovered, until the vegetables are tender and the juice has thickened. Add the vinegar and the remaining beans. Season with salt and pepper. Keep warm.

3. Cut the remaining leeks into fine julienne. Deep-fry in vegetable oil until crisp. Drain well on paper towels and season with salt.

4. Season the steaks with salt and pepper. Sear on both sides in a small amount of oil in a heated skillet; cook until done to taste. Remove the tying strings from the steaks and place 1 steak in the center of each serving plate; top with the fried leeks.

5. Stir the remaining 2 cups tomatoes into the beans. Spoon around the steaks. Garnish the beans with thyme leaves and cherry tomatoes. Serve immediately.

*When tomatoes are out of season use canned tomatoes and their juice for a total of 6 cups and add 1 tablespoon of dark brown sugar.

# FILETS MIGNONS WITH SAUCE ORIENTALE

3 cups Cabernet Sauvignon or Merlot
1 tablespoon cassis syrup or crème de cassis
1 piece star anise
1 tablespoon finely minced garlic
1 tablespoon finely minced fresh ginger
2 tablespoons soy sauce
1/4 teaspoon five-spice powder
1/2 cup demi-glace
beef stock
3 or 4 baking potatoes
olive oil
salt and freshly ground black pepper to taste
2 large leeks, white part only, finely julienned
vegetable oil for deep-frying
6 to 8 small filets mignons, trimmed, tied

1.   For the sauce, combine the Cabernet with the cassis syrup and star anise in a nonreactive saucepan. Cook until reduced by 1/3. Add the garlic and ginger. Cook until reduced to 1 cup. Stir in the soy sauce, five-spice powder and demi-glace. Bring just to a simmer and strain. Thin with a small amount of beef stock if necessary; the flavor will be very intense.

2.   Preheat the oven to 400 degrees. Peel the potatoes and cut into halves lengthwise. Cut the halves crosswise into slices 3/4 inch thick. Toss with a small amount of olive oil, salt and pepper in a bowl. Stand the slices on edge on a baking sheet. Roast for 25 minutes or until the potatoes begin to brown.

3.   Deep-fry the leeks in the vegetable oil just until they begin to brown. Drain on paper towels and season with salt. Set aside.

4.   Season the steaks with salt and pepper. Sear in a small amount of vegetable oil in a heated skillet for 3 to 5 minutes or until done to taste, testing with the point of a sharp knife.

5.   Remove the tying strings from the steaks and place each steak in the center of a warmed serving plate. Ladle the sauce over the steaks and arrange the potatoes in a spoke design around the steaks. Top with the fried leeks and serve immediately.

*Although many Asian seasonings work well with wine, the cuisines tend to produce dishes that are either too sweet, too salty, or too spicy. That is why I am an enthusiastic proponent of "fusion" dishes which combine Asian cuisine with western ingredients. Star anise is wonderful with Cabernet or Merlot, pointing up those hints of licorice flavor. The soy sauce provides a depth matching that of these wines, which I think comes from the fact that they are both fermented products.*

Serves Six to Eight

151

W I N E S  &

Very sweet and very rich desserts define American cooking perhaps more definitively than any other aspect of our cuisine. We love our desserts. This can create a problem when we add wine to the table. When you start tasting wine with desserts, it quickly becomes clear that the wine needs to be slightly sweeter than the food. Otherwise the wine will taste sour, thin, and/or bitter.

Dessert wines come in a wide range of sweetness. The most delicate are the sweet sparkling or still wines with fairly low alcohol. In the middle range are late harvest wines. The most intensely sweet and alcoholic are fortified wines.

Even those who love sweets may find the combination of very sweet desserts with very sweet dessert wines too much of a good thing. It becomes cloying on the palate. Fresh fruit desserts, nut tortes, or nut cookies are the best accompaniment to dessert wines, or a small bittersweet truffle with the Port. Coffee, tea, or water are the best choices for our famous American sweets. A cookbook without desserts is like a day without wine, so here are the desserts, with a beverage recommendation for each.

# D E S S E R T

# DESSERT RECIPES

# SPARKLING WINES AND DESSERT WINES

**Sparkling Wines:** There is a lot of confusion about sparkling wines, and at least some of the confusion is due to the fact that the first ones made were very sweet. Serving them with dessert was therefore appropriate, and certainly make a dramatic finish to a meal.

Sweet Champagnes made today will be marked on the label as Doux, the sweetest; Demi-Sec, medium sweet; or Sec, slightly sweet. Champagne, the sparkling wine made in the Champagne region of France, and sparkling wine, bubbly from any other region in the world, have evolved into a range of wines, most of them quite dry. It is a common mistake for a bride and groom to toast to their future with a dry Champagne and sweet wedding cake. This is definitely not a (food and wine) marriage with any hope of success.

All sparkling wines are quite high in acid. With dry sparkling wines, the best success in food pairing is to compare their styles to the still wine categories in this book. Most of the recipes in the Sauvignon Blanc chapter would be ideal for the driest bubblies. Consult the Rosé/Blush wine chapter for Rosé and blush or Blanc de Noirs sparkling wines. Some of the finer Champagnes have a yeasty and/or toasty richness that aligns very well with some Chardonnay recipes.

**Dessert Wines:** Dessert wine is a term that loosely describes a group of wines that are sweet enough to serve with dessert, or even as dessert. They fall into three categories.

*The first category* is comprised of wines that are sweet due to the fermentation being stopped by filtering out the yeast before all the sugar in the grapes can be converted to alcohol. The resulting wine is therefore lower in alcohol (7 percent to 9 percent is typical) and quite delicate. Muscat Canelli and Asti Spumante are good examples of this type.

*The second category is* late harvest wines. The grapes are left on the vines well beyond the normal harvesting time, allowing very high sugar levels to develop. Late harvest grapes become more concentrated from loss of water due to intentional drying, or the activity of the botrytis mold. These wines are very sweet, almost honey-like on the palate, with alcohols from 12 percent to 17 percent. Riesling, Gewürztraminer, and Zinfandel are the varieties most often made into late harvest wines.

*The third category is* fortified wine, which is made by adding pure alcohol to a partially fermented wine. This stops the fermentation by deactivating, or "killing" the yeasts, with the high alcohol level. As a result, we get Port and Cream (or sweet) Sherry, very sweet wines with alcohol levels as high as 24 percent.

Serves Eight

# CHILI-LIME SORBET

1 cup sugar
$1/2$ cup light corn syrup
zest of 1 lime
3 cups water
2 jalapeños, seeded, chopped
$2/3$ cup lime juice
2 egg whites
$1/4$ cup sugar

1. Combine 1 cup sugar, corn syrup, lime zest and water in a saucepan. Boil for 5 minutes. Remove from the heat and add the jalapeños and lime juice. Cool the mixture to room temperature.

2. Strain into a shallow metal pan. Freeze for 2 hours or until firm. Place a stainless steel mixer bowl in the freezer.

3. Beat the egg whites in another mixer bowl until foamy. Add $1/4$ cup sugar gradually and beat until soft peaks form.

4. Place the chilled lime mixture in the chilled bowl. Whip until broken but not slushy. Whip in $1/3$ of the egg whites; fold in the remaining egg whites.

5. Spoon into an ice cream freezer container. Freeze using the manufacturer's directions.

# APPLE GALETTES

3 large cooking apples, such as yellow Delicious,
Pippin or Granny Smith
1 pound puff pastry or 1 (2-sheet) package frozen puff pastry
2 tablespoons melted unsalted butter
6 tablespoons superfine sugar
¼ cup vegetable oil
¼ cup clarified butter
confectioners' sugar for garnish

1. Preheat the oven to 400 degrees. Peel the apples in thick even strokes and reserve the peels. Core the apples and cut into thin slices.

2. Roll out the pastry or defrost the frozen pastry sheets on a work surface. Cut 6 large circles using a saucer as a template. Place on a lightly greased baking sheet. Arrange the apple slices in a circular pattern on the pastry. Brush with melted butter and sprinkle with sugar. Bake for 30 to 35 minutes or until the pastry is golden brown and the edges of the apples begin to caramelize.

3. Cut the reserved apple peels into fine julienne. Fry in several batches in the vegetable oil and clarified butter just until light golden brown; peels will continue to cook and get darker after they are removed from the oil. Drain on paper towels.

4. Sprinkle the galettes with the fried apple peels and serve warm. Garnish with confectioners' sugar pressed through a fine strainer.

*Since this dessert is not overly sweet, you could enjoy a small glass of dessert wine with it. A late-harvest white wine, such as Sauterne, would be ideal.*

Serves Six

*I found this idea in an old cookbook from the Waldorf-Astoria Hotel to use for a 1950s theme party. Because the berries are not overly sweet and the sweetness is diffused by the wine, it does work well with a good fruity Rosé Champagne. I only recommend this dessert if you can get home-grown berries at the peak of season. This is one low-fat dessert no one will refuse!*

Serves Four to Six

---

# STRAWBERRIES AND RASPBERRIES IN ICED CHAMPAGNE

1 basket fresh strawberries
1 basket fresh raspberries
4 to 6 mint sprigs
1 bottle Rosé Champagne, iced

1. Chill 4 or 6 dessert bowls. Clean the berries by brushing them with paper towels or a pastry brush; do not wash unless they do not come clean with brushing.

2. Cut the strawberries into halves or into vertical slices if they are very large. Arrange the berries and mint in the chilled bowls just before serving.

3. Bring the desserts to the table with a bottle of ice cold Champagne. Pour a small amount of the Champagne over each dessert. Serve the remaining Champagne in Champagne flutes, or reward the chef with it later.

# APPLE TART WITH A POLENTA CRUST

CRUST
1/4 cup unsalted butter, softened
1/4 cup sugar
1/2 cup polenta
1 egg, at room temperature
1/4 teaspoon salt
3/4 cup flour

FILLING
4 pounds Gravenstein apples, or other cooking apples
2 tablespoons sugar
1 to 2 tablespoons lemon juice
2 tablespoons sugar
2 tablespoons unsalted butter

1. For the crust, preheat the oven to 350 degrees. Cream 1/4 cup butter and 1/4 cup sugar in a mixer bowl until light. Add the polenta, egg and salt and beat until smooth. Mix in the flour. Knead very lightly on a lightly floured surface. Wrap the dough and chill for 15 minutes or longer. Roll and fit into a buttered 10-inch tart pan. Bake for 8 to 9 minutes.

2. For the filling, increase the oven temperature to 375 degrees. Peel and core the apples and cut into halves. Cut enough of the apples into thin horizontal slices to measure about 3 cups. Toss with 2 tablespoons sugar and lemon juice in a bowl and reserve.

3. Chop the remaining apples coarsely. Cook, covered, in a heavy saucepan over low heat for 20 minutes or until tender. Add 2 tablespoons sugar and 2 tablespoons butter. Cook until the sauce thickens enough to hold its shape in the spoon. Purée in a food processor for a finer texture if desired. Cool to room temperature.

4. Spoon the sauce into the crust. Arrange the apple slices in a spiral over the top. Bake for 30 minutes or until the sliced apples are light brown. Serve warm.

*As you can see from the amount of sugar in this recipe, this is not an overly sweet dessert. If available, a late-harvest Chardonnay would be a perfect match, with the apple flavors usually found in this wine. However, almost any white dessert wine would be enjoyable, as long as the residual sugar is at least seven percent. If this information is not on the label, a knowledgeable wine merchant can identify these wines.*

Serves Six to Eight

*Fresh ripe peaches and raspberries are wonderful in combination but, to me, cooking them is a travesty. Here is my idea of how Pêche Melba really should be made. The fruit is just warmed, so all the fresh flavors still shine through. With the soft texture of the fruit and the cold temperature of the ice cream, I would not find dessert wines an appealing addition. If a beverage is called for, I would serve tea.*

Serves Four

# FRESH PEACH AND RASPBERRY GRATIN

2 ripe peaches
10 to 12 ounces fresh raspberries, or other berries in season
2 tablespoons cassis, black currant liqueur
2 tablespoons sugar
1/4 cup packed light brown sugar
vanilla ice cream

**1.** Plunge the peaches into boiling water for 15 seconds to loosen the skins. Peel, cut into halves and slice the peaches. Toss the raspberries with the cassis and sugar in a small bowl.

**2.** Mix the peaches and raspberries in a small nonreactive baking dish or individual gratin dishes; sprinkle with the brown sugar.

**3.** Preheat the broiler. Broil the fruit mixture for 2 to 5 minutes or just until the brown sugar melts. Serve immediately with ice cream.

# POLENTA FRUIT COBBLER

1 1/4 cups flour
1/2 cup cornmeal
1/2 cup polenta
1 tablespoon baking powder
1/4 cup sugar
1 teaspoon salt
6 tablespoons chilled butter, chopped
2 eggs
1/3 cup buttermilk
3/4 to 1 cup sugar, depending on the sweetness of the fruit
1/4 cup arrowroot
10 cups chopped fruit, such as apples, peaches,
plums, berries, rhubarb, or a mixture
1 cup whipping cream, whipped, or 1 pint vanilla ice cream
8 mint sprigs

1. For the polenta rounds, mix the flour, cornmeal, polenta, baking powder, 1/4 cup sugar and salt in a large bowl. Add the butter and mix by rubbing with the fingertips until the mixture resembles coarse meal.

2. Beat the eggs in a bowl until frothy. Add the buttermilk and mix well. Stir into the dry ingredients and mix to form a dough; dough will be quite wet. Roll 1/2 inch thick on a floured surface and cut with a 2- to 3-inch cookie cutter.

3. For the filling, mix 3/4 to 1 cup sugar and the arrowroot in a saucepan. Add the fruit and toss to coat well. Cook until the fruit begins to be tender. Pour into a 9x12-inch baking dish.

4. Preheat the oven to 400 degrees. Arrange the polenta biscuits evenly over the top of the fruit mixture. Bake for 20 to 25 minutes or until the tops are light brown. Serve warm, topped with whipped cream or ice cream and the sprigs of mint.

*A late-harvest white wine is sweet enough to go well with this cobbler. If you do decide to serve one, I would keep the ice cream or whipped cream as a minor note, so the wine can be the cold refreshing contrast to the warm dessert. This makes a few more polenta biscuits than you need; bake them separately and serve for breakfast.*

Serves Eight

Serves Eight

# GINGER CRÈME BRÛLÉE

1 (2-inch) piece fresh ginger
1 quart whipping cream
8 large egg yolks
3/4 cup sugar*

1. Peel the ginger and slice into 1/16-inch rounds. Combine with the cream in a saucepan. Bring just to a simmer and remove from the heat. Steep for 20 minutes.

2. Beat the egg yolks with 1/2 cup of the sugar in a bowl until thick and pale yellow. Add the heated cream in small amounts, stirring to mix well. Strain into a bowl and skim off any foam which may form on top.

3. Preheat the oven to 325 degrees. Pour the custard into eight 6-ounce custard cups. Place in a baking pan filled halfway with warm water; place a sheet of waxed paper over the top. Bake for 45 to 55 minutes or until the custard begins to set. Remove from the baking pan and chill until firm.

4. Preheat the broiler. Sprinkle the tops of the custard with the remaining 1/4 cup sugar. Arrange the custard cups in a pan filled with ice. Broil just until caramelized and brown.** Place on serving plates and serve immediately.

*I prefer the flavor of brown sugar for the caramelizing, but the brown sugar must be dried out in the oven and repulverized, as it otherwise has too much moisture to caramelize properly.

** A small propane blow torch may be used to caramelize the topping. They are available at a reasonable price at most hardware stores. They are very easy to operate, and are truly the easiest way to caramelize the sugar without melting the custard.

# Walnut Shortcakes with Fresh Figs and Pears

4 ounces walnuts, toasted, chopped
2 cups flour
1 tablespoon baking powder
1/2 teaspoon salt
1/4 cup sugar
1/2 cup chilled unsalted butter, chopped
2/3 cup plus 1 tablespoon half-and-half
1 tablespoon sugar
1/4 cup water
1 cup Pernod, Champagne or Vin Santo
1/3 cup sugar
8 to 12 fresh Mission or Turkey figs, depending on size*
6 ripe pears, such as Comice, Bartlett, Red or Asian
whipped cream and mint for garnish

1. For the shortcakes, combine the walnuts, flour, baking powder, salt and 1/4 cup sugar in a food processor container. Add the butter and pulse until it is reduced to 1/8-inch pieces. Add 2/3 cup half-and-half and process just until the mixture forms a dough.

2. Roll 1 inch thick on a floured board. Cut with a 2-inch cookie cutter and place on a parchment-lined baking sheet. Chill for 30 minutes or longer.

3. Preheat the oven to 350 degrees. Brush the tops of the shortcakes with 1 tablespoon half-and-half and sprinkle with 1 tablespoon sugar. Bake for 20 minutes or until light brown.

4. For the filling, combine the water, wine and 1/3 cup sugar in a saucepan. Cook for 30 minutes or until syrupy. Cut the figs into quarters lengthwise. Add to the hot syrup. Add the pears just before serving.

5. Split the shortcakes and place the bottom halves on the serving plates. Fill with the fruit and replace the tops. Garnish with whipped cream and mint.

* When fresh figs are not in season, substitute dried figs. Cut them into 4 pieces and cook with the syrup for the entire 30 minutes.

*This is a great dessert to serve with a dessert wine. It is not overly sweet, and the dryness of the walnut biscuits makes an excellent foil for the wine. A Muscat, a late-harvest white, a demi-sec or slightly sweet Champagne, or an Italian Vin Santo would all be suitable.*

Serves Eight

*Ginger flavors make an excellent foil for cream sherries and aged tawny ports. Gingerbread or ginger cookies are simple and appropriate. For a more formal presentation, try this tart. The proportion of pecans to filling is greater than in a typical pecan pie, so it is not icky sweet.*

Serves Twelve

---

# PECAN TART IN A GINGER COOKIE CRUST

### CRUST
1 cup (8 ounces) unsalted butter
1/2 cup sugar
2 tablespoons grated orange peel
1 tablespoon finely minced fresh ginger
2 cups flour    1 teaspoon ground ginger
2 teaspoons cinnamon
1/4 teaspoon ground cloves
1/4 teaspoon salt

### FILLING
2 eggs    3/4 cup sugar
2 tablespoons melted unsalted butter
3/4 cup light corn syrup
1/4 teaspoon salt
2 tablespoons Cognac or brandy
1 cup coarsely chopped pecans
1 to 2 cups pecan halves
whipped cream and mint sprigs for garnish

1. For the crust, combine the butter and sugar in a mixer bowl. Mix with a paddle at low speed for 3 minutes. Add the orange peel and fresh ginger and mix well. Add the flour, ground ginger, cinnamon, cloves and salt and mix to form a dough.

2. Press most of the dough into a greased 11-inch tart pan; wrap the leftover dough in plastic wrap. Chill the crust and wrapped dough for 30 minutes.

3. Preheat the oven to 350 degrees. Roll the leftover dough on a floured surface and cut into gingerbread men or other decorative shapes. Place on a baking sheet. Bake for 10 to 12 minutes or until golden brown. Bake the crust for 12 minutes. Cool on a wire rack.

4. For the filling, beat the eggs, sugar, melted butter, corn syrup and salt in a bowl. Stir in the Cognac and chopped pecans. Pour into the cooled crust. Arrange the pecan halves in a decorative pattern over the top of the filling. Bake for 30 to 35 minutes or until a knife inserted in the filling comes out clean.

5. Cut into wedges to serve. Garnish with whipped cream and mint. Serve with a ginger cookie.

# HENNESSY CHOCOLATE PECAN TART

pastry for a single 10-inch tart shell
2 eggs
1/2 cup sugar
1/2 cup light corn syrup
1/4 teaspoon salt
2 tablespoons butter
1 ounce unsweetened chocolate
1 cup chopped pecans
2 tablespoons Hennessy Cognac
1 to 2 cups pecan halves

1. Preheat the oven to 450 degrees. Line a 10-inch tart pan with the pastry. Bake for 5 to 7 minutes. Cool on a wire rack. Reduce the oven temperature to 350 degrees.

2. Beat the eggs, sugar, corn syrup and salt in a mixer bowl. Melt the butter and chocolate in a saucepan and mix until smooth. Add to the egg mixture with the chopped pecans and Cognac and mix well.

3. Pour the filling into the pastry. Arrange the pecan halves in a decorative pattern over the filling. Bake at 350 degrees for 35 to 40 minutes or until the pastry is golden brown and a knife inserted in the filling comes out clean.

*A traditional pecan pie was the starting point for this dessert. I bumped up the proportion of pecans to filling, added the unsweetened chocolate, and used Cognac instead of vanilla. The result is not so achingly sweet as the original, but it's still a pretty intense dessert experience. Serve it with coffee and a tiny glass of Cognac.*

Serves Eight

*Chocolate chip cookies are magic; they always disappear in a flash. To make my favorite version, I have made two changes to the classic Toll House recipe. The first is the addition of some chopped bittersweet chocolate as well as the semisweet chips, which reduces the sweetness of the cookie. The second is forming the dough into rolls which are frozen and cut into 1/4-inch slices to bake. This results in a thin crisp cookie, which is my preference. Cold milk, coffee, or tea is best with these, as they still pack a wallop of sugar.*

Yields Five Dozen

# CHOCOLATE CHIP COOKIES

1 cup unsalted butter, softened
3/4 cup sugar
3/4 cup packed light brown sugar
2 large eggs
1 teaspoon vanilla extract
2 1/4 cups flour
1 teaspoon baking soda
1 teaspoon salt
1 cup chopped pecans
1 cup chopped bittersweet chocolate
2 cups (12 ounces) semisweet chocolate chips

1. Cream the butter in a mixer bowl until light. Add the sugar and brown sugar and beat until fluffy. Beat in the eggs 1 at a time. Add the vanilla and mix well.

2. Mix the flour, baking soda and salt together. Add to the creamed mixture and mix well. Stir in the chopped pecans, the chopped chocolate and chocolate chips.

3. Shape the dough into 2-inch rolls and wrap in plastic wrap. Freeze for 1 hour or longer.*

4. Preheat the oven to 375 degrees. Cut the rolls into 1/4-inch to 3/8-inch slices and place on a greased or parchment-lined cookie sheet. Bake for 8 to 10 minutes or just until the edges begin to brown. Cool on the cookie sheet, loosening first with a spatula if parchment is not used. Store in an airtight container, if you can keep any long enough to store.

*For fresh-baked cookies with a minimun
of time and effort, slice and bake the
amount of cookies you need and store
the rest in the freezer.

# GINGER COOKIES

1 cup unsalted butter, softened
1 1/2 cups sugar
1 egg
4 teaspoons grated orange peel
2 tablespoons dark corn syrup
3 cups flour
2 teaspoons baking soda
1 teaspoon ginger
2 teaspoons cinnamon
1/2 teaspoon ground cloves
1/2 teaspoon salt
currants for decoration

1. Cream the butter and sugar in a mixer bowl until light. Add the egg and orange peel and mix well. Add the corn syrup and beat until fluffy.

2. Sift the flour, baking soda, ginger, cinnamon, cloves and salt together. Add to the creamed mixture 1/4 at a time, mixing well after each addition. Divide into 4 portions. Wrap in plastic wrap and chill until firm.

3. Preheat the oven to 350 degrees. Roll the chilled dough 1 portion at a time to less than 1/4-inch thickness on a floured surface; the thinner the cookies, the crisper they will be. Cut into decorative shapes. Decorate gingerbread men with currants for eyes, etc.

4. Place 1 inch apart on ungreased cookie sheets. Bake for 8 to 10 minutes or just until the cookies begin to brown. Remove to a wire rack to cool. Store in an airtight container.

*This is a recipe of unknown origin, passed on from family to family. I got it from my sister, who used it to make gingerbread men for her children at Christmas. I pass it on to you, with an acknowledgement to the unknown creator. Serve them with a late-harvest white wine, unless you make gingerbread men. In that case, you must serve them with cold milk or hot spiced apple cider.*

Yields Two Dozen Gingerbread Men
or
Four Dozen Cookies

*This fancy palm leaf cookie is often served as a petit four in France. With frozen puff pastry available in the grocery, these are fairly simple to make and not overly sweet. This makes them a nice accompaniment to any dessert wine you prefer.*

Yields Two Dozen Three-Inch Cookies

# PALMIERS

1 small sheet frozen puff pastry
2 to 4 cups sugar

**1.** Thaw the pastry until it is pliable but still cold. Sprinkle 1/8 inch sugar in an area slightly larger than the pastry on a work surface.

**2.** Place the pastry on the prepared work surface and roll lengthwise to increase the length. Fold lengthwise into thirds, folding the left side over the center and the right side over the left. Sprinkle the work surface with sugar again and repeat the rolling and folding process.

**3.** Sprinkle the work surface with sugar again and roll the pastry into a rectangle 1/4 inch thick. Fold the 2 long sides to meet in the center; fold into halves lengthwise to make 4 layers of dough. Press together and cut crosswise into 3/8-inch slices.

**4.** Place the slices cut side up on a parchment-lined baking sheet with space between for expansion. Cover and chill in the refrigerator.

**5.** Preheat the oven to 450 degrees. Bake the palmiers for 5 minutes or until the bottoms have caramelized. Turn and bake for 3 to 5 minutes longer to caramelize the other side. Remove to a wire rack to cool. Store in an airtight container.

# PECAN BALLS

2 cups pecans, toasted
2 tablespoons sugar
1 cup unsalted butter, softened
1/4 cup sugar
1 teaspoon vanilla extract
2 cups flour
1/2 teaspoon salt
confectioners' sugar for coating

1. Preheat the oven to 300 degrees. Process the pecans with 2 tablespoons sugar in a food processor until ground.

2. Cream the butter in a mixer bowl until light. Add 1/4 cup sugar and beat until fluffy. Beat in the vanilla. Add the flour, salt and ground pecan mixture and mix well.

3. Shape into small balls and place on a parchment-lined baking sheet. Bake for 25 minutes or until light brown. Roll in confectioners' sugar while still warm.

*I always thought that these cookies were quintessentially American until I started delving into the cuisines of the world. Then I discovered Russian Tea Cakes and Mexican Wedding Cakes, and, basically, they are all the same cookie. Even though the cookie itself is not very sweet, the powerful hit of the confectioners' sugar coating makes coffee or tea the best accompaniment.*

Yields Three Dozen

The mousse for this recipe is very intense. The recipe is essentially Julia Child's—my favorite of all time—except I have used bittersweet chocolate instead of the German's sweet chocolate she specifies. The caramelized sugar on the phyllo rounds adds enough sweetness to balance the less sweet chocolate. Though a good port could stand up to this, even I, with my sweet tooth, find it an excessive amount of sugar. Coffee or tea please.

Serves Twelve to Fourteen

# CHOCOLATE NAPOLEONS

4 egg yolks
3/4 cup superfine sugar
1/4 cup Grand Marnier or other orange brandy
6 ounces bittersweet chocolate, chopped
1/4 cup brewed strong coffee
3/4 cup (6 ounces) unsalted butter, softened, cut into pieces
4 egg whites
2 tablespoons sugar
1 recipe Napoleon Pastries (page 171)
1 1/2 cups whipping cream, whipped
mint sprigs and baking cocoa for garnish

1. For the mousse, beat the egg yolks with the superfine sugar in a bowl until the mixture is pale and thickened to the consistency of mayonnaise. Add the Grand Marnier and place over simmering water. Heat until the sugar dissolves, beating constantly. Place the bowl in ice water and continue to beat until thickened and cool.

2. Combine the chocolate and coffee in a microwave-safe bowl. Microwave on High for 1 minute; stir to blend well. Stir in the softened butter gradually. Add to the egg yolk mixture and mix well.

3. Beat the egg whites in a mixer bowl until foamy. Add 2 tablespoons sugar and beat until stiff, but not dry, peaks form. Fold into the chocolate mixture 1/3 at a time. Chill, covered, in the refrigerator.

4. To assemble the Napoleons, place a small spoonful of the mousse on each dessert plate and place a pastry round on it. Spoon mousse onto the round, taking care that it does not extend over the edge. Add another pastry round and a spoonful of whipped cream. Top with a final pastry round and a dab of whipped cream. Garnish with a mint sprig and cocoa sifted over a fork. Serve immediately.

Note: Although this recipe makes a large amount of mousse, it really is difficult to make a small quantity successfully. It does keep well for several days. For variety, try serving the leftovers on top of vanilla ice cream. A restaurant in my distant past, long gone and name forgotten, used to serve this and call it Vamousse; it must have been the sixties!

# NAPOLEON PASTRIES

8 or 9 sheets phyllo dough
¼ cup melted unsalted butter
sugar

1. Preheat the oven to 400 degrees. Cut the phyllo sheets into 6 pieces. Stack the phyllo sheets to keep from drying out. Brush the top layer lightly with melted butter and sprinkle with sugar.

2. Place an entremet ring on a parchment-lined baking sheet. Gather up the buttered and sugared piece of phyllo and press it into the bottom of the ring and remove the ring. Repeat with the remaining sheets of phyllo.

3. Bake for 7 minutes or until golden brown, checking after about 5 minutes and rotating the pans if necessary for even browning. Cool to room temperature.

*Using phyllo instead of puff pastry lightens these Napoleon pastries considerably. Make an entremet ring to shape the pastry by removing both the top and bottom of a tuna can and washing well.*

Serves Twelve to Fourteen

171

# INDEX

173

*Chameleon recipes, which have been
adapted to pair with another wine.